Gypsies and Travellers
in their own words

'Romanichals rokker about
their kushti merripen'

'Pavees thoryin' about
crushin' on'

Words and Pictures of Travelling Life

Compiled and Edited by

Peter Saunders Jim Clarke
Sally Kendall Anna Lee Sakie Lee Freda Matthews

LEEDS
CITY COUNCIL

DEPARTMENT OF
EUCATION

© 2000

Leeds Travellers Education Service Publishing Group

Published by

Leeds Travellers Education Service
West Park Centre
Spen Lane
LS16 5BE
Telephone: 0113 274 8050

Compiled and Edited by
Peter Sa⋯⋯rs
Jim Cla.
Sally Kenda
Anna Lee
Sakie Lee
Freda Matthews

Development and Production
Jim Clarke

The views expressed in this publication are not necessarily those of the publisher

ISBN 0 950 8029 99

Designed and Typeset by Leeds Education Publications and Promotions   Floor 10 West Merrion House   110 Merrion Centre   Leeds LS2 8DT

Foreword

I was very pleased and honoured to be asked to write a foreword to this lovely 'story' book in the true sense. It is a simply delightful book to read. This book is a compendium of real life stories told by Gypsies and Travellers and spanning the best part of the twentieth century. It represents a substantial resource of oral history which will prove increasingly valuable as source material for local archival studies, research and, not least, to inform teachers about Gypsy and Traveller history and culture and aid in the preparation of curriculum materials for improving the quality and accuracy of knowledge for all children.

These personal and genuinely honest stories are beautifully illustrated with associated pictorial records and thus also bringing together a vast and unique collection of hitherto unseen photographic material.

Although each story has its own individual character reflective of the special man or woman relating it, there are also some common themes, which must contribute to a more informed and sympathetic understanding of the history and culture of Gypsies and Travellers, both locally and nationally. The delight, interest and celebration of family shines through all the testimonies and acceptance, affection, protection and a concern for not only the extended family, but also for the common good of the wider human family. There is too, an understanding and empathy with all who struggle to make a living to survive, while at the same time a justifiable pride in the occupational ingenuity and adaptability of Gypsies and Travellers. Despite the uniformly nostalgic recognition and acceptance of changing times, their stories also tell of the continuing strength and confidence in Gypsy and Traveller ethnic and cultural identity, their language, their previous nomadic lifestyles and the love of all things equestrian. This will come as a shock to those who are too ready to say that there are no 'true' Gypsies these days.

There are also those common strands coming through the stories which are more humbling, yet poignant for the 'settled' population. We know from history scholars that Gypsies and Travellers have suffered centuries of racial abuse and gross social exclusion, including an act of genocide in the Tudor period. Through these stories we are given a glimpse of how they have survived such a hostile social and physical environment. Patience, adaptability, forbearance, a sense of h   .., and even forgiveness, have been part of the repertoire of skills developed so naturally by an endu   .ople.

Although most of the stories speak of a lo   ror the open road and the need to travel for fairs or work, it is also very clear that the level of nomadism has been strongly influenced by the impatient action of local authorities and the police. These negative and shameful revelations are matched by the very poor access these families have had to schools and basic educational achievements. The suggestion that the current policy of some authorities re the eviction of Gypsy and Traveller families is tantamount to institutional child abuse, is offered some credence in these pages.

But these personal stories have not been told to provide material for history scholars, or teachers, but are personal testimonies of proud, happy, joyful and dignified lives, which are worthy of telling, and must stand alone as statements of truth and rich human experience.

This book will make an invaluable addition to the growing body of evidence which daily informs us that the Gypsies and Travellers of Europe are the hidden jewel in the European crown. If the non-Gypsy people of Europe can come to terms with their wilful race hatred, persecution and discrimination of Gypsies and Travellers, then we shall be well equipped to face the new and challenging demands of globalism in the next millennium. In reading the pages of this book we shall have made significant headway on this essential journey.

Arthur Ivatts

Former Her Majesty's Inspector for the Education of Gypsy and Traveller children in England 1986-1998

Methodology

We had worked with Traveller families for a long time and had enjoyed their stories and histories as they were told whilst visiting Sites and camps over the years. We spoke with some families about doing a book about Travellers' lives and the idea was well received. We applied for funding from Leeds City Council and the Department for Education and Employment and received a grant to do the book.

We set up a Publishing Group which comprised: Peter - from Leeds Travellers Education Service, Sally - an Adult Education worker for Travellers, Freda - who had worked for Leeds Travellers Education Service and had done a great deal of research into Travellers' history, Anna - who is a Gypsy and had worked for Leeds Travellers Education Service for three years, and Sakie - Anna's husband, who is also a Gypsy and an excellent Romanes speaker.

The reason that there are few stories available is that the majority of Gypsies and Travellers being nomadic communities have not developed literacy as the settled communities have. We wanted Gypsies and Travellers to tell their own story and decided to tape them and have them transcribed word for word. We drew up a list of areas we hoped to cover and framed questions around these to help keep the stories going and make sure we covered everything we felt was important.

We printed leaflets about the Book we were doing and passed these to all the Gypsies and Travellers we knew and spoke to and encouraged as many people to join in as possible. We hoped to have about ten stories and get photographs from the families to enrich the book and give a personal touch.

We asked Jim Clarke from Leeds Department of Education Publications & Promotions to do portrait photographs of all the storytellers in their own homes. These were to be the first phographs of the storyteller and would give us a strong image of who was telling their story.

We encouraged Traveller children to be involved by drawing illustrations to be incorporated into the book.

The taped stories were transcribed. We then took the stories and without adding or changing any words we edited the stories to help them flow a little better and to draw together particular themes or ideas that had arisen through the story. We wanted them to read like stories rather than a series of questions and answers, so we edited out all the questions and just let the stories flow. We then took the edited versions back to the storytellers and read them through to make sure they were happy with the edited version. Any amendments were done there and then with the storyteller present to approve the changes.

Since the project began there has been great enthusiasm and interest shown by many people and particularly Gypsies and Travellers, who have contributed so much that the book is now more than three times its originally intended size! We now have sixteen main stories. In between each story we have either: photographs of a family or individual; photographs of Camps or the Site in Leeds; photographs and the history of three Northern Fairs.

We have had lots of photographs loaned to us from many different people who wanted to help us enrich the book. We owe a great deal to all those who have lent us treasured family pictures whose very uniqueness brings this book to life. They may not all be technically perfect, but their inclusion makes evocative and invaluable contributions.

The Book has taken a lot longer than we envisaged and yet it has been enriched over this time from 1996 to 2000 by many contributions that have been so interesting that we did not want to miss them out.

Leeds Travellers Education Service Publishing Group

Preface

These stories represent just some of the experiences of Gypsies and Travellers living in Leeds.

In their own words, Gypsies and Travellers provide fascinating insights into their lives, from early in this century to the present day. These are personal histories and viewpoints but collectively they create a vivid picture of life within the Gypsy and Traveller communities and the radical changes those communities have experienced over the past century. Many tell of the difficulties caused by misunderstanding and discrimination which Gypsies and Travellers have faced in the past and which in many ways they continue to face to this day.

It is hoped that Gypsies, Travellers and the settled community will use this book as a resource to promote and enhance the cultural identity and self-determination of all Travelling communities. It is also hoped that it will be used to promote Gypsies' and Travellers' positive self-understanding as ethnic groups and to improve the knowledge and appreciation of different cultures. In addition, it is hoped that this book will go a little way in improving the settled communities' understanding of Gypsy and Traveller culture thus creating opportunities for greater empathy to exist between the communities.

Whilst providing an insight into everyday life, the stories tell of both personal and cultural survival. They show some of the lighter aspects of life, highlighting Gypsies' and Travellers' resourcefulness and ingenuity.

The collection both reflects and celebrates the diversity Gypsies and Travellers bring to English society and shows the communities' declaration of pride in their culture.

Some of the photographs included within the text are described in Romanes or Cant. We hope that the use of these languages will encourage interest in them and enable Gypsies and Travellers to enjoy this book and contribute in helping non-Gypsies and non-Travellers understand the richness of their language, if they so wish.

Romanes and Cant are ancient languages with different roots. Most Gypsies and Travellers will have a fair knowledge of one or both languages. English syntax is mostly used with Romanes or Cant words. Romanes is a Sanskrit language and is thought to have its roots in northern India, from where it is believed Gypsies originated over a thousand years ago. Cant, also known as Gammon or Shelta, is hundreds of years old and originated in Ireland. Shakespeare refers to this language in a speech of Prince Hal when he boasts of

'...being able to drink with any Tynker in his own language.'

(Henry IV Act 2 scene 4)

Acknowledgements

The Leeds Travellers Education Service Publishing Group would like to thank the following for the support they have given to us whilst preparing this publication:-

Special thanks to - all the Gypsies and Travellers of Leeds who have made us so welcome, especially those who have shared their stories with us and all the young Gypsies and Travellers who have provided us with their brilliant drawings including:

Anne Boswell	Mary Doran	Lisa Joyce	Scarlet Nicholson	Alfie Reynolds
Chantel Boswell	Thomas Doran	Jamie Lee Kelby	Shannon Nicholson	Benny Reynolds
Joe Boswell	Ambrose Gaskin	Amber Kindon	Tommy Nicholson	Charmaine Reynolds
Kathleen Boswell	Violet Gil	Ann-Marie Lowther	Helen Louise Pattison	Kathleen Smith
Michael Boswell	Bridgie Hanrahan	Ben Lowther	Rocky Pattison	Amos Smith
Pa Boswell	John Hanrahan	Samboy Lowther	Tammy Marie Pattison	Becky Smith
Felix Connors	Teresa Hanrahan	Andy Mitchell	Budweiser Price	Chantel Smith
Robert Doherty	Charlotte James	David Mitchell	Dawn Price	Michael Smith
Tommy Doherty	Joe James	Miley Moloney	Donna Price	Selina Smith
Anne Doran	Kizzy James	Sakewell Nicholson	John Price	Tom Smith
				Dougie Ward

Grateful thanks for funding to:

Leeds City Council

The Department for Education and Employment (DfEE)

European Commission

Socrates

Comenius Action 2, Multicultural Resources For All
for contributing towards the printing costs

Personal thanks to:

Yvette Gallagher, Leeds Department of Community Benefits and Rights, for her advice in the initial stages of planning the book

Mike Robertshaw, Ronel Bekker, Dawn Wood, Peter Costa and Gary Nethercott, Leeds Department of Education, for their support and encouragement

Everyone at Leeds Travellers Education Service who have encouraged and enabled us to make this book a possibility - Stephen Clark, Jacky Glass, Sue Gold, Dianne Greenhow, Sue Itzinger, Veronica Keon, Anne Leach, Fiona Lovelace, Sentabell Mabbott, Claire Norris and Carol Ward

Ray Russell for the book cover design

Judith Rushworth for transcribing all the stories

Helen Ford, Paul Hudson, Jim Clarke, Leeds Education Publications and Promotions, for the design, layout, editing, typesetting, image editing, proofreading, pre-press preparations and production coordination

Gareth Hewitson-May for his generous support and encouragement during the final stages of production

Everyone at New World Images Design and Print involved in making the book a reality

Acknowledgements

Photographic Sources

From Gypsy and Traveller Families

Peter Saunders, Leeds Travellers Education Service

Jim Clarke, Leeds Education, Publications and Promotions

David Atkinson - Lee Gap Fair in 1965 (p77)

Mandy Farrar - 'Roadside Stop Bradford' (p166 Ada, p224 Jim Nicholson)

John Niven - Mary Ann Smith on Topcliffe Fair (p134)

Claire Norris - Cottingley Springs (p236)

Len Sanderson - Camp at Birkby Brow Wood, Morley in 1957 (p63)

David Smith - Righteous Price (p104)

Bobbie Syrett - Camps in Leeds 1970's (p170, 171, 172)

Dave Thomas - Roy Gentle (p159), Appleby Fair (p 206, 207, 208) and Katie Nicholson (p224)

Bradford Education Service for Travelling Children - 'Johnny Eagle' in Anna Lee's story (p86)

University of Liverpool Special Collections - Topcliffe Fair (p134 Mary-Ann Smith) - thanks to Katy Hooper

Thirsk Museum - Topcliffe Fair (p130, 131, 136) - thanks to the curator, J. Cooper Harding.

Permission to Photograph

Castle Museum, York and Thwaites Mills, Leeds, for permission to photograph their Bill Wright's wagons and use the motifs for artwork.

Rev. Terry King, Vicar of St. Mary's Church, Woodkirk, for access to the church and permission to photograph for the story of Lee Gap Fair.

Permission to use Published Materials

Maureen Baker and the United Caribbean Association for the use of the two stories (Bob James and Sara Ann Morrison) researched and published in the Heritage Journal

David & Charles Publishers, for permission to use line drawings of Gypsy wagons by Denis E. Harvey published in 'The English Gypsy Caravan - Its Origins, Builders, Technology & Conservation' by C. H. Ward-Jackson & Denis E. Harvey (1972)

Barrie Law, Romany Gypsy Photograph Collection (Ada at Appleby p168 and Camp in Leeds 30's p60)

Yorkshire Post Newspapers for permission to use archive photographs
- First day at Leeds school for Traveller children (p11)
- Camps in Leeds (p61, 107, 114, 115, 179, 180, 232, 234)
- 1968 Eviction (p116-119)
- Topcliffe Fair (p137)

Yorkshire Life, for permission to use published materials from their archives
- cover photograph of October 1962, Jimmy Berry painting the Bill Wright's wagon at the Castle Museum, York (p147) which was from an original colour transparency by Arthur Taylor
- Lee Gap Fair (p76)

Labour Campaign for Traveller's Rights for permission to use the photograph of 'The Morrison Family' taken by Paula Sollaway (p90)

We have tried, as far as possible, to be accurate with names, places and dates. We apologise for any inadvertent errors or omissions. Peter Saunders, of The Leeds Travellers Education Service, would welcome further information or comment on any aspect of the contents of the book. His contact details are on page (i).

Contents

Content Strands

Individual Stories (16)

Between the Stories

Camps and Sites (4)

Characters (3)

Evictions (2)

Fairs (3)

Families (7)

Story One   Tommy Doherty   2

School - Marking the road - The 'Black March' - The Specials - Stewartstown - Hard times - Campaigning - England - Leeds - Civil rights - Stopping evictions - Site in Leeds - Education - Retribution - Cant - Marriage - Traditions

The Doran Family   16

Story Two   Bobby James   22

My ancestors - Earning a living - School - The workhouse - Prize fighting - Fairs - Horses - Women dealing - New laws - Travelling - Roadside camps - Farm work - Sites - Not living in a house - The countryside

The Buxton Family   30

Story Three   Eileen James   32

Travelling - Harassment - School - Sites - Marriage - Cleaning up - Improving the site - Trailers - Old age - Wakes - Mourning - Religion - Language - Children

The Stewart Family   40

Story Four   Tilly Kelby   48

Travelling - School - Jobs - Work - Camps - Sites - Water - Evictions - Prejudice - Country people - Differences - Racism - Changing tastes - Trailers - Packing down - Ear piercing - The site - Improvements

Contents

Contents

x

Contents

Introduction

Gypsies and Travellers have always lived on the margins of society, when they have not been ignored or forgotten, mostly they have been misunderstood. The Gypsy and Traveller culture is based on a strong oral history, thus the majority of written documentation in existence is derived from non-Gypsy and non-Traveller sources. It is hoped that these stories will go some way in redressing this imbalance.

The stories relate to a period in time which has been an important one in history for all people. Changes in technology, mechanisation and legislation have transformed all our lives, including those of Gypsies and Travellers. The collection highlights the adaptability of the Gypsy and Travelling communities - communities which, according to settled commentators, have been dying out since the nineteenth century. The Gypsy and Traveller cultures have survived and developed, despite a long history of persecution and controlling legislation. Anti-Gypsy and anti-Traveller legislation may be seen as an historical process of exclusion and spatial control, evident in this country since the arrival of Gypsies and Travellers in the sixteenth century.

The first written reference to Gypsies and Travellers in Leeds can be found in the Parish Register of 1572, when Anthony Smawleye, the 'Egyptian' had his daughter Elizabeth baptised in the Leeds Parish Church. Called Egyptians (eventually corrupted to 'Gypsy') because of their perceived origins in Egypt, these early Gypsies and Travellers were soon discriminated against by strict laws passed under Henry VIII. These laws expelled Gypsies from the country and banned others from entering under pain of death.

In 1562 settled people found associating with Gypsies were also liable to the death penalty because Gypsies were seen as 'foreigners' and potential spies. Also massive unemployment and fear of civil unrest at that time led to the passing of anti-vagrancy legislation with the aim of containing the wandering masses, including Gypsies and Travellers.

Today we can still see the legacy of Gypsy and Traveller encampments dating back to the seventeenth century in street names in and around Leeds. Gypsy Lane near Middleton Woods, Gypsy Hill and Gypsy Mead in Woodlesford, Gypsy Wood Close in Colton and Blackman Lane off Woodhouse Lane near the University of Leeds. In fact, Blackman Close near there was mentioned in the Survey of the Manor of Leeds in 1612. Tinkler Lees (Gypsies and Travellers were often called Tinklers or Tinkers), also mentioned in that same survey was situated near Pontefract Lane in the area now called Cross Green where there are Gypsy and Traveller camps today.

There were also van towns in the city in the late nineteenth century and up to the 1930's. The Brickfields at Armley had one hundred and fifty vans, tents and huts on the ground between Armley Town Street and Stanningley Road. When they were finally evicted in 1934 many of the residents had been there for fifty years or more and records from a neighbouring school show of Gypsy children attending as early as 1902.

Introduction

Some of the stories in the collection reflect the lives of Gypsies and Travellers in the early years of the century, spent in yards around Hunslet and Holbeck. After the Second World War these yards started to disappear due to housing and roadway redevelopment. Gypsies and Travellers were finding it increasingly difficult to find places to camp. We have included sections on camps, evictions and site development in Leeds to illustrate this difficulty of finding 'somewhere to stop' particularly over the last fifty years.

This situation and the legal framework made it virtually impossible for Gypsies and Travellers to camp on private land unless the owner had obtained a licence for a designated caravan site. The increasing scarcity of land to camp on led to many violent evictions, increasing the impetus for the establishment of a number of pressure groups. These groups were made up of Gypsies, Travellers and others from outside the Travelling communities who were campaigning for site provision.

Eventually this came in the shape of the 1968 Caravan Sites Act. However, whilst the Act ensured that all local authorities in England had a legal obligation to provide sites for *'Gypsies, residing in or resorting to their area'*, the legislation also increased local authorities' power to evict those Gypsies and Travellers not resident on official sites.

The first official Leeds site at Cottingley Springs was built in 1969, it provided sixteen pitches for the two hundred or so Gypsy and Traveller families resorting to the area. Additions were not made to this inadequate provision until the two present sites, providing fifty-six pitches, were built in 1987 and 1990. This provision was reduced in 1998 to forty-six pitches and is still insufficient to accommodate the Gypsy and Traveller families of Leeds. This lack of provision has been exacerbated by the removal of the local authority's legal obligation to provide sites, contained in the Criminal Justice Act. In addition, planning legislation ensures that it remains extremely difficult for Gypsies and Travellers to make their own site provision, as applications for planning permission are consistently refused.

We also include ten photographic collections from families and individuals. Each of these photographs is decribed in their own words. Throughout the stories, Fairs play an important 'marker' in the lives of all Gypsies and Travellers. We have therefore included a brief history and a photographic portrayal of three Northern Fairs - Appleby, Lee Gap and Topley.

We hope you enjoy this book with its sixteen main stories and the themes of camps and sites, family photographic collections and the history of local Fairs which interweave the stories.

The Leeds Travellers Education Service
West Park Centre   Spen Lane   Leeds   LS16 5BE   Telephone: 0113   274 8050

Dedication

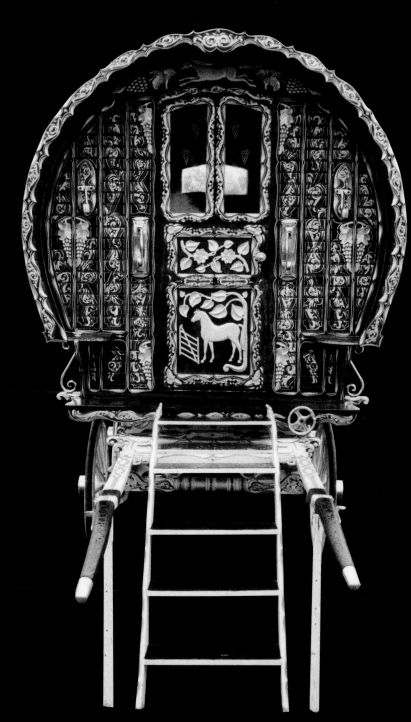

This book is dedicated to

All Gypsies and Travellers

and especially to

Bobby James, Annie Kindon and Bobby Lee

who unfortunately never saw this book completed

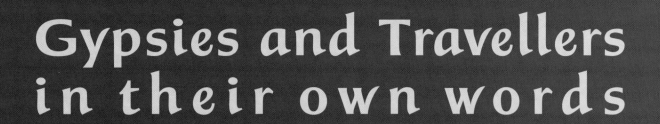

Gypsies and Travellers in their own words

It would be kushti to dell wava kuvva some of the wava romani rokkerpen.

I hope the Romani people kums the romani lil.

The puri rokkerpen is probably dui dish birshes.

It would be kushti for the chavies to jun the puri rokkerpen and sor the romani lavs.

Duva rokkerpen sarbi kushti harjun through the chairas.

Dell to dell buka sarsti moss on your family yokker.

Kushti buk.

Sakie Lee

1

Tommy Doherty

I was born in Dublin by accident, not by choice. My mother went up there and I was born in 1937. On my Register of Birth it says - *"Caravan, so-and-so"*. Funny thing is that I was born in Dublin and never, ever lived there. My father always stuck to the North of Ireland.

...tells his own story

I think I got my kick from me grandmother. Now she wasn't a Traveller. I really remember her. She was my mother's mother. She was, we would call her a 'country woman'. She was called Winnie Burns, and me grandfather went off with her as a young girl, he was a boy then. She was not a Traveller, but me grandfather was. They were all Travellers bar her. I'm sure she'd be cast as an outcast.

In them days you (Travellers) were dirt, you were nobody. If you went to hospital you were put to one side, we were classed as dirt. My parents had less education than me. They were married very young - my mother was sixteen or seventeen, my father was eighteen. I had it bad in my time, but they had it twice as bad.

I only spent one day in school - me and me brother, Bobby went to school. In the morning me mother and father brought us down to school, and I could smell the chalk, I could smell the milk, I could smell the classroom and I was looking forward to getting some of this milk - in little bottles, you know and sitting down. The teacher was a lovely woman, she was a grey-haired woman. Suddenly these two policemen come in, RUC men come in, and talked to her and pointed down to us, and said, not through her fault, *"You have to go, boys, you're moving on."* That's the only education I ever got - half a day. So we went back with the policeman, me father had already tackled up and was ready to go. Me mother was hawking all day - she'd come back and find we'd moved.

Me father marked the road. We leave marks. Indians had the same rules, marking where they'd been. And we had the same sense as that; we'd mark the road. We'd put a bit of grass down going that way. Come to a crossroads, and we'd put the grass one way. It wouldn't blow away, we'd find something hard on the road, so it wouldn't blow away. Or a bit of flour down, if you had any, throw it on the floor, and they'd find yer. Me mother, she'd walk miles and miles to find us. So that was one very sad thing for me mother. We really suffered back there. There was no security - nothing like that.

If you were on the road in Ireland there wasn't a lot of traffic around, and the weather seemed different then - there was always warm weather. If my father saw a bike coming in the distance and saw a cap shining, he would go and hide. Me father was a very strange man, he was very nervous. He thought it was an RUC officer and his experience of them in the past was terrifying. He'd go and hide in a field till they'd gone. It could be a postman, only one man on his own.

There were certain places you could go and the worst time of the year if you were in Northern Ireland, was the 12th July. You had to get out of the area, if you were in a Protestant area, you had to move out of there immediately and get to a safe area. A safe place was Newry, part of Newry was safe. Armagh city was safe - it was a Catholic area.

If you were in Portadown when they came back from the black march, well you were number one target. They'd come back drunk and kick everybody on the place, break everybody up. I remember as kids they'd make us sing *"The Sash My Father Wore"*, we had to sing it. The women were there, the men had to go away and hide in the fields, but the women never went away and we'd move out of that area immediately.

There was some good people. I remember one farmer, he and his wife, they'd no children and they'd give you jobs picking spuds every year from the field. They were Protestants, but they were nice people. They were called Johnsons. They gave us all the best of food. So this really bad winter, it was 1947, they gave us

this big shed to go into. The Specials came and they fired these shots over the house. It was a Protestant house. So my father said *"You'd better go and get the Police, you, there's going to be trouble here."*

It was called New Mills, this place, there was a little river with a bridge and a telephone box. I had, I think, 4d to ring the police. I put the money in the box - it was pouring down with rain. I was ringing 100 to get the operator and the door opened and a gun come through the door as I stood there. He said *"Come out you Papish B——. What are you doing in the phone box?"* I said *"Ringing the police. Someone fired shots."* He said *"We fired 'em at yer. Get down the road you —."*

I remember the noise of the bullet, the bar being pulled back. I was terrified. My father left next morning. My mother begged him to stay - he wouldn't stay. As I was walking near that house, I heard all the bars being pulled back on the guns. They never fired them, but it was the same feeling you would get if they did fire them.

Then we took a house in a place called Stewartstown. A one bedroom house, one room upstairs. At the back of the house was an open drain. We were the only Travellers there, it was an open sewer all the way down, and everybody had TB in the street. We stayed there for a while, but my father couldn't settle in a house. This priest came and he said *"Why don't you go on to Social Security. You at least get some kind of food?"*

My uncles (they're all dead now) all went down to sign on at the dole office. They got £5 a week for signing on. They used to get the money over the counter - £5, a big white £5 note. I used to go with them every week to pick this money up, as a child. We went one morning and the police were waiting for us, said we couldn't sign on any more, must leave the town. So that finished.

That was the only money my father would claim in his life, I remember that. It was bad but we survived it. We all survived it.

Then we were in a place called Bessbrook, we were starving with hunger, we'd no food, we were desperate. So we'd go up the field and pick up spuds, they were in a pit covered with clay and straw to keep the frost off, you know, so every night we'd go and pick them - not a lot - a bag full, and that's all we had, the spuds and a bit of buttermilk and butter and salt.

One night the farmer came down with a police van, I'll never forget this. The pan of spuds was on, and this fellah said to me cousin - *"You've a nice pot of spuds on, Patrick."* *"I have"*, he says. *"Can I have one?"* *"Of course you can have one"*, he says. He took a penknife out of his pocket and took a spud and he cut it in half and he said *"You're arrested, come on."* The farmer had been down the day before and put a black thread through his spuds, put a needle through, and cut it at each end, all the spuds in that pit. Me cousin was four months in prison. I'll never forget that.

Then we were stopping at a place called Larne, where all the boats come in from Scotland and me aunt, Mary Ellen Ward, was, you could call it hawking the houses, they call it begging back there. She was hawking the whole street and this chemist man gave her a penny, one penny. Before she got to the end of the street she was arrested, for begging. The chemist man done that. He gave her a penny then called the policeman over and she was taken to Armagh prison, she did one month in prison there. Oh they really were hard on Travellers.

They had awful tricks, Travellers. When I was a young boy, the farmer came down the road in the morning to you and he'd say *"Oh my God, how do you get your money, how do you make your money? You got nice horses, nice ponies and traps there."* No cars then. He'd say *"Well, we make our own money, sir."* And the farmer would fall for it, as God is my judge. And he'd become very greedy, the old bastard would say *"How do you do it?"* He said *"Well, you have to buy the silver first."* *"How much does silver cost?"* *"£20."* That was a lot of money. So Tom would get a lump of lead, from a Church somewhere, melt it down into a block, wrap it in brown paper and tie it, leave it in a shop, say *"I'll come for that tomorrow."* He'd leave it in a hardware shop; he'd never use another shop. So they'd bring the farmer into town next day and *"Look, I need £20 to buy the stuff, but you stay outside."*

He'd pick the parcel up - obviously it was his parcel. He'd go back then to the tent, the camp, and he'd have a box, a bit bigger than your tape recorder, and what Tom would do - it would be all full of fancy studs and things, and he'd go to the bank and get 2 new half-crowns, and he'd put them in the bottom - in a little drawer. Well, the farmer would come down and look at him melting this silver (it was only lead) and pour it into a little hole, and he'd put a drop of water in first, and the smoke come up. He'd wait 10 minutes now, and he'd pull the drawer open - *"There you are. Two new half-crowns."* *"God, I'll buy that box off yer!"*

Greedy bastard, and when he found out he was fiddled he'd go to the guards. In my opinion, he should have been arrested too, shouldn't he, 'cos he was committing the fraud, wasn't he? And the police would pull him on the roadside and make him come back and get his money back. To me, I couldn't tell then, I was too young, but now I realise it, the farmer should be charged too. He was doing the counterfeiting, and because it come unstuck he went to the guards, but the guard being a farmer himself... *"Oh, I'll follow them bastards on the road."*

Then you'd get another farmer on the road, he'd come down - we call them 'Lonely boys, lonely men' - they'd come down the road. He'd be a bit thick in the head, he'd say *"How do you get your women?"* As soon as they heard that immediately *"Well, come and live with us, and get one of them yourself."* *"Can I come and live with you?"* *"Right."* They knew he'd money, you see. *"Bring whatever money you've got, and bits of things, and you'll be welcome."* They'd take him along and the poor fellow would drag along the whole way. When the money was gone he was left behind.

I remember one fellow, a big man he was, his hands as big as that table, he was, I'll never forget him. And all his money - I think it was £100 then, £100 was like a fortune. Big heavy money. And he said *"I'll have all your money from you now, John,* (We'll call him John, I don't remember what his name was) *and this woman's ready for you next week."* *"Alright then, fair enough."* A big, thick farmer. So when the money would be gone, they said to him *"Look, there's 2 shillings. Go down the road and bring some milk and a loaf of bread up."* Well, it would be 4 mile. They get in and go on with horses and carts and they leave him there. Oh, they knew all the tricks.

But then a fellow called old Tom Connors, he would never have a horse, only an ass, a donkey, wouldn't have a horse given to him. I remember one occasion, everybody had a horse in this road, but Tom had a grey ass, a white ass. This farmer come down. He says *"Tom, I'm looking for a good ass, but I wouldn't have a grey one given to me. Get me a brown ass and I'll give you £4."* You could get grey ones for half-a-crown, 2 shillings. Tom said *"I'll get you one tomorrow, I'm going down to such-and-such a place."*

He goes to the chemist shop, and got potash and dyed his ass brown. So in the morning he says *"Right. There's your ass for yer."* The farmer give him the £4. The man would go off. It rained three days later - all

washed off. The farmer come and said *"Some bastard's swapped me ass in the field and left me a grey one!"*

Old Tom was famous for that. They weren't cruel, but they were very wise.

To get the horse lively and kicking about, what they used to do - nettles up the horse's arse. You know they sting you, don't they? Or mustard, if they could afford it. The horse would be dancing up to the sky. Obvious. When they were away, the horse was just dead.

My father was a tinsmith. He'd make the tins, me and me mother would go and sell them round the farms. The shops would give you orders. He'd make a bucket, a basin, a jug for milking cows in, and he'd sell them.

As time went on the Government brought new laws out, about seams in the buckets and chrome buckets. The Health people said we can't put milk in a bucket with a crease, (what they call a seam in the bucket). Me father could do nothing then. That was about 1950-53. His trade was finished. They wouldn't buy anything off you. They could buy a plastic bucket or a chrome bucket.

So he left Ireland and moved to Birmingham looking for work, with all the other men. But it was no time at all before they came back over again. There was signs in Birmingham then - I remember me father saying when he come back - *"Irish don't apply for jobs here"*.

He died in Leeds but he couldn't settle here - didn't like it over here. He'd nothing to be proud of about Ireland, because Ireland was really bad to us back there.

When being a tinsmith finished then we sold rags, then scrap, then there was a phase on feathers, feather beds, after that they went on to recycling car batteries, that was a chore. Travellers would pick all the rubbish up and resell it again, which they do today anyway. As time went by they went on to tarmac, building, antiques, the whole cycle.

Travellers can change - they're not stuck with one thing. If someone tomorrow morning said they should look for red beetles, they'd get them, they'd find a way of getting them. They're like that - they're very economic that way.

In 1953 in Ireland, I was about 16. My father was very afraid of the police. The police could come and do all sorts to you at night. They'd come at night - particularly at night. And they'd wait till the darkness come. We were all stopped at Portadown, which is a very Protestant place, down a long narrow road. It was fruit country, we picked the fruit that hung over the road from the branches. About 9 o'clock a car pulled up with these four blokes, all carrying rifles, dressed in police uniforms. They wanted us to leave there and then. My father said *"We'll go now"*, he was very afraid, and my cousin, he'd have walked out too. I was only 16 and it was too late, so I said *"No, we're not going."*

So they had guns out, they wouldn't use it as a gun, but hit you in the face with them. So me cousin got hit in the mouth, he had blood everywhere. So I ran to the police station, two miles away. As he opened the door, the policeman, I says *"Can you help us?"* He said *"Who are you?"* So I told him who I was. There was a big coal fire on and a policeman reading a paper. He had to get his tee-shirt on. So I said *"We're out at the caravans and the police are beating us up."* He said *"Oh hang on a second..."* He beat me across the face in the police station, blood poured out of me. Chucked me out the door.

I remembered a man called Mr. Kells, Cruelty Inspector for Children. He was a Protestant, too, but he wasn't a bad man. So I banged on his door. He came out in his pyjamas. I was covered in blood, just a

nose bleed, but a nose bleed can be bad, can't it? He took me in the house and I told him what happened, that we'd been beaten and I went to see the police and the police beat me up. He went to the phone and he said to me *"Go home now, Tommy. Everything will be O.K."* Which it was, they were all gone, the police were all gone, but it was a shambles, it was all wrecked.

Then the campaign started, really and truly. We went to all these bishops and priests in Ireland, the Travellers, and told them about these Specials. They got a senator to take it up in Stormont, Belfast. There was a small bit in the Belfast Telegraph about me, about complaining about the police. This bishop, called the same name as me, Doherty, he said *"The best advice I can give you is to get out of here as quick as you can. If they get their hands on you they'll kill you..."* So I went to Glasgow. I was only about 16 at the time.

I was over there for a while and then went back again to Ireland. I started campaigning again but it wasn't successful. There was no chance you could win over there. You couldn't meet anybody, you couldn't even talk to clergy, or they listen to you but they won't go further than that. There was one priest, called Father McSean, he used to help us. He used to give us money when he couldn't afford it and he helped us out a lot.

So we moved and we travelled all over England. On one occasion in Manchester,

NORTHERN IRELAND 1959

We were on the Antrim coast in the North of Ireland. You can see the sea at White Abbey. We had an old 'Trugeon' van and a 'Vanguard' car to tow the trailers for us all. They were good times.

KNOCK IN COUNTY MAYO 1959

We were going to the shrine and we were having a bite to eat. There is Kathleen Maughan; Biddy, me wife; George, me dad; Eileen, me brother's wife and Martin Cawley, me uncle.

on the Great Lancashire Road, a great wide road, we all pulled in with the wagons and trailers. There was a family with us, they'd 3 or 4 big girls, grown girls. There was a police car (a big old Zephyr, like you used to see in 'Z Cars') parked down the road and a policeman with it. We didn't heed it and he moved away.

So the girls went down the road for a walk and apparently he made an obscene suggestion to the girls to get in the car with him. So they came and told us. One of the men went down and confronted the policeman and complained. That was the worst he could have done. The police came in hundreds in vans and *'slaughtered'* us on the 'Lancs Road'.

ON THE ROADSIDE IN 1959
We were stoppin' between Sheffield and Barnsley at the time. The group includes me brother Bobby and Eileen, Philly and Paddy Cawley, and Winnie Doherty.

NEWCASTLE 1960
I took this photo of all me brothers stoppin' there.

BARNSLEY 1961
Stoppin' on the old coal mine outside town at the time.

I come to Leeds because travelling was really bad in the 50's and 60's. I wasn't going to get involved again, because my wife said *"You're going to get killed. You're going to get murdered."*

One day I was going down Kirkstall Road, before they altered it, and I saw a family being moved on by the police and they rough handled them. My nerves got the better of me and I got out of the car - and confronted the police.

After that I started to campaign really strong for Travellers in Leeds, and when they were attempting an eviction in Leeds I went and stopped it. Nine times out of ten we stopped it. We organised the Travellers not to move for them. We got Travellers to leave their vehicles there. It grew so big that the Yorkshire Post got on to it, and I was called from John O'Groats to Lands End to Travellers; it was a full time job then. They called me the King of the Gypsies. And it's been all me own money. I never had any money from Travellers. Never asked any money from Councils. That went on for about three or four years. I approached the Council on a site for Travellers. They wouldn't hear tell of it. No way. No site for Gypsies in Leeds.

About 1965 Leeds University got involved. We started a campaign. We had a number we could ring at Leeds University Union. One number to ring - and we'd have hundreds of students out in minutes. And that stopped the police moving the Travellers on.

I would use delay tactics. I remember I went to Preston in Lancashire, one time. There were about forty Travellers there and we were in a bit of nowhere - like a sewer farm it was. But they'd nowhere to go. Again the police come down there heavy-handed, and the Council men come

Bug away the feen anosher is goin' to corrip us if we don't crush on.

(Cant)

A ROADSIDE CAMP IN MEANWOOD, LEEDS 1966

The council officer is moving the family on from one unofficial camp to another. There are no 'official' sites for Travellers in Leeds at this time.

down too. I arrived, anyway. The police had known me in Preston. I organised them not to move and the Travellers stood against the police. So the police had a brilliant idea: they'd bring the bulldozers down and block us all in - forty families, you couldn't see them all in this tip. I had a brainstorm, I got over the tip and went to the nearest Fire Station and asked for the Fire Prevention Officer. I said:

"Look, we have a problem, we've got Gypsies on here, they've been blocked in. Can you see if there's any safety for Ambulance or Fire Engine to get in."

The Fire Officer come down, he looked around like and then he said to the police:

"Look, as far as I'm concerned, if there's an emergency, that's a community of people, I can't get a Fire Engine in there, and therefore you must make a space for them to get through."

That was a great victory that day, everybody was up in arms, clapping the police, and the bulldozers had to move away the earth to make a gap. All the Council came down next day and said:

"We cannot accommodate all of you, but we will accept twenty of your families."

Wherever I was, there's been a site made, there's one there too, now.

POLICE IN BIRMINGHAM

Police action during an eviction in Birmingham in the 1960's

In Leeds the Town Clerk more or less sympathised with me that the Travellers should have somewhere to go. A fellow called Pat Crotty (he's now deceased) he was a solicitor in Leeds, he was all for the Travellers and there was also a few of the councillors for the Travellers.

Then the Caravan Act came in '68, which gave us some power. They set several sites in Leeds all over the place, from a sewer farm right down to a cattle market, anywhere. Well, some of the Travellers wouldn't go to certain places, you know. *"I won't go there. I won't go there."*

So eventually they pointed out a temporary site at Cottingley Springs, that was for six months, and they said *"You can go on a temporary basis."* All the local farmers round there got a petition up saying:

"If Gypsies move in, we move out."

It never happened. The only people that never signed the petition were the Jewish people; the Rabbi at the Jewish Cemetery wouldn't sign the petition. Had he signed it we wouldn't have got our site. Thank God the man didn't go for it. So the site was opened there temporary. Now it's the permanent site, Number One and Number Two sites, so that was the kicking off point in Leeds.

But the Travellers still wasn't being educated. We approached all the schools in Leeds and they wouldn't let the children start schools. So we went down to Leeds Education Department with all the Travellers' children. I said:

"According to the 1944 Education Act, you're not doing your job. These children need education."

The press was there, Granada Television, (there was no Yorkshire Television then) and the BBC covered it, and it embarrassed them. So there were places at ten schools for Travellers immediately.

It's school time for the Travelling children

First day of school for these children of caravanners camping on cleared sites in the Holbeck area.

They were received at Bewerley Street Mixed Junior and Infants School.

A score of children, aged between five and eleven years old, attended school in Leeds today for the first time.

For most of them, it was the first time any member of the family for generations had crossed the threshold of any educational institution.

Yorkshire Evening Post 18.4.1967

'They wouldn't let any of the children in the schools.

They said they were full, there was no room, so we went down to the Education Offices by the Town Hall with all the children.

They had a meeting and promised that they would have places for all the children in twenty-four hours.

The Evening Post took the photographs of the children as they started school.

This was the beginning of Education for Travellers.'

Tommy Doherty

On our first day at school we were frightened to go in.

After a bit of persuasion we went in, through the big doors.

FRANCE IN SUMMER 1967

Tommy Doherty with Vanko Rouda, who was the President of The International Committee together with other committee members: Mehmet Sakirovic and Cuna (Yugoslavia); Lola (Spain); Venni, Grattan and Corin.

They changed in Leeds, but I paid the price. One night in Leeds in Tong Road, me and me brother was coming home, walking up the street, up Tong Road, and we'd just been to the fish shop for some fish and chips. Now I hadn't drunk for six months, on the pledge, wasn't drinking, and two motorbikes went down the road - two noddies, like little motorbikes, and they spotted me near the church which is now the Sikh Temple on Tong Road. They turned their bikes round in the road, said *"Doherty."* They said *"You put your fingers up at me, didn't you?"* I said *"I did not."* He said *"Oh, you did, you bastard yer."*

So he come off his bike, hit me with a truncheon just there, near my eye. Bobby, my brother, was handcuffed to the railings, I wasn't. They laid into me with these truncheons, these two policemen. Somebody run up to me house and me mother came running down and me wife went down. Well, me mother threw herself on top of me in the road to save me. The police van arrived then. She was arrested, me mother. She was bad with her chest with asthma, so they were kicking her in the Black Maria, these policemen. They weren't picking on Bobby because they didn't know who Bobby was.

So we were both brought into the Town Hall. I was brought to the counter. I was held by the hair this way, back that way, and if I opened my mouth I got slapped in the face. And they referred to me as 'The King'.

"The King's here, right?"

I could hear me Mother screaming, but I went into a cell, a police cell, and these two policemen came into the cell, and they lit into me. The walls were covered in blood from end to end. Everywhere blood. I asked for help. My nose was busted, my eye was busted - I've still got the mark there - the end of my chin there was busted. They sent for a doctor, wouldn't take me to the hospital, and he put some sticking plaster on.

The next morning Pat Crotty came in - he was a solicitor - I knew to ask for him. He was a councillor in Leeds Council. But he was there to see me, but they wanted me out of the cell, put me in a clean cell. I wouldn't come out of the cell. I said *"I'm not moving, I want to be here when the solicitor comes."*

So four big policemen comes in, drags you out. Then I saw two women go in, two women in blue overalls, clean the cell up. I was brought into court; we had case for the jury there and then, so we had witnesses, the landlord of the pub called Kathleen, she was a witness; a vicar up the road was a witness, come with his car; the woman from the fish and chip shop was a witness. We went to court anyway. My mother was found Not Guilty, my brother was found Not Guilty. I remember the magistrate saying to us, *"Well, I don't count heads, I count the police."*

I was fined £1 and no charge against the police.

That was about 1969. But the police today are not too bad, they're different altogether now. They've changed.

SHEFFIELD IN 1969

The families were being evicted, so we organised and got a site opened and schooling provided for all of the children.

Picture anosha feens an' bewers on it. The pavees are buggin' munya for us. (Cant)

TRAVELLERS IN STRASBOURG FLYING THE EUROPEAN FLAG

This is taken in Strasbourg. We went to Court there in 1968.

We were all giving evidence to The Court of Human Rights about the treatment of Travellers.

That's me and the doctor - a French Traveller - who was giving evidence on our behalf.

The British Consulate denied all harassment of Gypsies, but we showed a film to the Committee and they were convinced. It proved we were right in what we were saying.

The film was called "An Outlaw's Life" and was made by the 'World In Action' team.

The camera was hidden in the trailers in a camp in Birmingham.

The film shows the police coming in buses. They lined up at the side and baton charged all the trailers.

It proved at Strasbourg that it did take place.

The Caravan Bill went through Parliament after this.

Traveller's own language is Irish Cant. It is very old, and I don't know where it's come from. I've tried to find out meself, and scholars have tried to find out. It goes back a long way. People say that Travellers were caused by 'The Famine' in Ireland. We weren't - the Famine was one period, but there were Travellers before that. I've been to Spain and there's Travellers there who carry on the Travellers' ways we had in Ireland - tinsmiths - that continues in Spain to this day. But not in Ireland, because the trade is a museum piece in Ireland now. If you ask a young Irish Traveller about it now, I don't think he'd be able to tell yer.

The rules, even of marriage, is all changed now. One time it was all arranged marriages; you couldn't bring a woman back and say you wanted to get married - it was all arranged for you. She could be a film star or she could be Frankenstein.

Back in Ireland both families would go to the pub for a drink and they'd say *"Oh your Mick can marry my Mary."* And you wouldn't think anything about it. Young boys fifteen or sixteen playing football or 'Tig' or 'Cowboys and Indians' and they'd say *"Come up here, I want yer. You get married to her."*

I should say the rules began to fade in the 1950's. Travellers became more advanced then, they'd meet girls in pubs and dances, and they'd come to the father. But they arrange one or two back in Ireland. Meet at certain places and arrange marriage, but very rare.

Travellers always had music. That was a famous thing. They had folk singing, and they'd sing songs. They'd go back for years and there was no end to them. They'd wind on, the women would start then. Then they're shaking hands, that was the rule, that they had to shake hands. And that would go on for hours and hours.

There's a lot of things have gone for good. Tradition has gone. Travellers had manners then. They've no manners now. They were ruled by one word, and it was a good thing in one way to be ruled. But it's all different today. Today, it's all *"I've got more than you."*

Travellers years ago would help one another, very clannish to one another, but now they won't. If you were back in the Free State and you were poor, some'at had happened, or your horse was killed or your wife died, they'd all help yer out. That's all gone. You've to borrow from them now and give it back to them. Then they'd collect for yer and just give it to yer - end of story.

There's different rules today, different principles. All the young family, me son, find Ireland strange. When you go back to Ireland from here, and you've been away for a while, they won't accept you very well. It's a clannish thing. It's been handed down for years. It's wearing off now, as education goes along.

Well, the kids today won't know anything about travelling, will they? They won't know what the word means. The word we use now - we go camping. We don't say that word - we go travelling.

The young ones, they don't know the difference - it's history to them.

The Doran Family

Me Grandfather, Dan Doran, in Graignamanagh, County Kilkenny, Ireland, back in 1921.

He is making a tin can, that was his trade. He had his own shop next to the Guard's barracks.

He used to go delivering his tinware with the donkey cart, all over the roads in County Kilkenny and County Wexford.

He was a well-known old Travelling man.

Bill Doran

This is me sister Joanna and Johnny Connors, her husband, with all the children.

Fak, Nanny, Natie, Josie and Eileen. It was taken in New Ross, back in Ireland in 1947.

It was all wagons and horses those days.

Bill Doran

This was taken in Scotland in 1948.

It was on Springburn, a stopping place for Travellers in Glasgow.

There's Biddy Maughan, with Sonnyboy, Snowy, Ada and Betty Gentle.

We had all come over from Ireland together.

Bill Doran

...in the olden days

Red Patsy and Katie Doran, my Mam and Dad, having a drink in the 'Black Bull' at Doncaster in 1957.

We were all camping on 'The Wagonfields' at the racecourse for the St. Ledger meeting.

Bill Doran

This was also in the 'Black Bull' in the Market Place in Doncaster at the time of the St. Ledger back in the sixties.

That's my mother and father, Katie and Red Patsy, with Harold Stanley, Grey Badge. He used to drive horses for my brother, Paddy and some other Travellers.

There's old Tommy Smith, Alfie Dear, old Jackie Cunningham, Andra's Dad, Essie Ayres sitting next to me brother Dan.

Bill Doran

The Doran Family

This is me aunt, Mary Connors, the Copper Kettle's mother holding a child on a camp back in the sixties.

Bill Doran

The water company, Midland Water, went round all the houses in a little blue van with a loud hailer on top. They told everyone that if they gave any water to the Travellers their own water would be cut off.

There was notices on all the shop and pub doors "No Gypsies or Travellers allowed".

At that time there was no protection against this racial discrimination.

Tommy Doherty

My mother, Katie Doran is with Tommy Doherty's mother, Sarah, holding Joseph, one of Tommy's brothers, and there is Kathleen, my brother Paddy and Mary's daughter.

They were stopping on a camp in Birmingham in 1961, they called it the Robin Hood camp, it was by a wood.

That's my Bedford van with all the chrome, that was the fashion of the day.

Bill Doran

This is me and my son Jim when he was one, back in 1963.

We were stopping on an old ground.

You can see the old Bedford van that Bill used to go hawking with.

Janie Doran

...sixties memories

This is Pa and Jim Doran, me sons, taken in 1964 in Great Yarmouth. They are sitting with their pup on the front of the Austin Cambridge pickup, 'a gentleman's classic'.

Bill Doran

Me Mam, Katie, with my eldest sister, Josie, hanging out the washing on a bright summer's morning in Sweet Street, Holbeck, Leeds, in 1966.

Bill Doran

This is an old camp in Leeds, in 1969.

They were pulling the old houses down, off Lady Pit Lane, Beeston, and we got stopping.

There is me with me children and me brother Whack and me brother Johnny's wife, Dowdie.

We were stopping with Weenie and Patsy Brazil and the Morrisons.

Bill Doran

This is me Dad, Jimmy Dolan, with Joe Lowther, David McMillan, who was married to our Kitty, and friends in Middlesborough Irish Centre in 1969.

Me Dad was captain of 'Cavan Gaelic Football Team' for seven years and took the team to America and won, back in the thirties.

He was from Belturbet in County Cavan.

Janie Doran

The Doran Family

This is meself, Janie and the whole family in 1974.

There's Jim, Pa, William, Dan, Tommy, Kathleen and Janie.

This was took in Hunslet, Leeds, on the very day that William and Dan had made their Confirmation at church.

Bill Doran

This is a family gathering, having a drinking party at the 'Dock Green' pub in Leeds in 1977. There is me brother Paddy, Jacob Lowther, my brother-in-law, Tom Connors and Mandi Lowther with his son, Jimmy. There's Johnny Purcell, Shorty Connors, another brother-in-law, Jimmy and Paddy Moloney, Paddy Maughan, known as Paddy de Bar, Jimmy Mulvanney, young Danny Connors and Tom Connors, young Jim Doran, The Cock Johnny's son, and Coco.

Bill Doran

This is a family photograph of the Dorans, Connors and Cashes. Everyone has got together for Julie and Coco's wedding in the late seventies. Old Jimmy Doran and Maggie are there. I'm in the middle next to Duck Connors. My wife, Janie, is in the middle with daughter Janie. There is Danny Six and Boy, Jerry Mike and young Johnny Cash, Heavy Duty Ned and my sister, Margaret, Buttons, Billy, my brother Paddy's son, Shorty and Kitty, Paddy Cash and Billy Connors.

Bill Doran

This is John Rooney, the Irish piper, playing a selection of reels and hornpipes on the Irish Uillean pipes.

He is playing for the 'The Hen', Johnny Doran's sons and Dinkey Delaney's boys. These boys are all related to the late Johnny and Felix Doran, the two great Irish pipers.

It was in a pub in Hemel Hempstead near London in 1988.

The last time we heard John Rooney play locally was at the Victoria pub in Sheepscar, Leeds.

We had some great night's entertainment and the local lads still talk about him.

Bill Doran

21

Bobby James

A person can't help what they are, they don't ask to come into the world, but I think that every person should be proud of what they are. I don't care what nationality, you should be proud of what you are, your ancestors. All my old people were Gypsy people and I were proud of them all. I am proud of being a Gypsy myself.

...telling his story

I loved my old gran, I never remembered my grandfather, but my old grannie she was over a hundred when she died and she used to pull handcarts when she was a young woman. She used to pull scouring stone, you won't know what that is; it's a piece of, like, a yellow stone, what they used to do their flags on houses. They used to have steps, and they used to do their steps with it and she used to go out selling that. Because she had a big family to fetch up and 'cos my grandfather left my grannie like before I were born and all that, and she used to pull a handcart all over the country selling it. It was hard. It was hard enough for us having no father, I mean I had nobody to advise me, because I was thirteen when my dad died.

My father used to do a lot of fighting in the ring, or out of the ring, you know, Geordie James, he was a prize fighter. He also worked on farms and things like that you know. Stooking corn and tatty picking, sugar beet picking, mangel picking, you know. But the main money was made through prize fighting. My mum used to go out hawking. Well, door-to-door peddling, you know, but there wasn't a lot of money in them days so you had to do farm work to survive.

All the breed in me were fighting men. They had to fight to eat in them days because there was no money you see. Yeah, my dad used to take me to fights. And every Sunday he'd make a ring and he'd stick me and my brother in, well I were two year older than him and he used to come in, he's dead now is my brother, he'd come in hammer and tongs and I'd lose my temper and give a little bit and dad said, *"you're a big guy you!"* I had to spar with him you know. And I'll tell you he didn't pull his hands. He used to hit me and my head used to shudder. Well it made a man out of me, it were no good him babying me and maybe it was a good job he didn't, as I wouldn't have been able to do what I did do when he'd gone.

I went to school very, very little. I went to Ingram Road for about 3 weeks. See when we used to go to school we had a bad life – it were *'Gypsy, Gypsy can't afford to pay your rent'*, and all this kind of thing. Cock or hen – I'm cock of this school, are you hen? Well you couldn't say you was hen, so you fought the cock of the school didn't you. Well that was it and that stopped it. But you used to get that *'Gypsy, Gypsy, Gypsy.'* It used to make you wild. I mean if you cut us red blood comes out, cut you red blood comes out, put that blood on a piece of white paper you can't say that's out of you and that's out of me, it's all the same blood isn't it!

In my dad's day they used to train at Thirsk. Well there is a racecourse there, but it's the other side of Thirsk where they used to train. My uncles, my dad's cousins, they used to train one another, and they'd walk to Newcastle from Thirsk, 'cos there was no transport in them days, it was all leg work. And they'd fight at Newcastle, they'd come down to Pontefract and they'd fight at Pontefract, back to West Hartlepool, that's where my father come from, and they'd fight there. And then they'd go back home, they'd train up again until the next time.

They had the gloves on in the rings. Outside the ring it were bare knuckles, no gloves. At the showgrounds, in them days there'd be a young fellow on to take all-comers and you'd get in with that man that was taking all-comers, or they'd make a make-up fight and you'd go in to whoever it was, you see. And you'd fight, you'd maybe get a pound, which was a lot of money in them days. And you'd done your best. If you lost you didn't get anything, so you couldn't afford to lose. The reason I did it were more or less to get money for my mother, 'cos I mean there was no social in them days, you went in the workhouse if you had no money then.

1950 LONG AGO
Me Mam and me cousin Dinah together with her two nephews Eddie and Billy. I think it was in 1950.

1970 STRAWBERRY FIELDS
This is me and Margaret and our son, Bennie. We were picking strawberries down in Wisbech. You had to be in the fields early and work the straight rows, they called them 'stints'. It was how we used to make a living in the summertime.

Oh, there was a lot that went in the workhouse, I mean it used to be over Holbeck Moor at that time. Well when you had no money, you couldn't pay your rent, and no food, they used to put you in. They had to scrub floors, and do washing, the men had to do gardening to grow vegetables and that's how they went on. A lot of householders, I never knowed any Travelling people to go in, but householders did. I mean it was the last resort for them. There were nowhere else for them. As I say there was no social then. So they went in there. And I believe they fetched social out, and then they done away with the workhouses.

Well we never thought of going in the workhouse. I mean we had a better chance than the householders. How should I say, we could go and get a rabbit so we wouldn't go hungry, you know, we'd have a dog, we'd get rabbits and doing work on farms we got tatties and things, you know what I mean. But I mean the poor people in the houses, they didn't do that.

My mother used to catch a bus, when we were little kids, to Tadcaster, we'd work in the farm, we'd get potatoes and we'd put clay on them, put them in the fire and at dinner time they was cooked and we'd have them.

I mean everything was rationed, if you had a million pound you couldn't have bought food because it wasn't in the shops to buy. And there wasn't such a thing as cafes, not for the working class. And that's how we lived, we'd roast tatties, if we had a bit of bread it was shared out. Bread was rationed you didn't get a lot.

Story Two

To get extra money I'd go boxing and what not, fighting anybody. No malice at all. You'd finish up friends with that man, you know. I've finished with men that I've fought and been pals, well some of them's dead now, and never had a wrong word. And if you have a bit of malice against them and you have a fight and then you shake hands because you've beat them or he might have beat you or whatever, you know. But there's no poison in a fight; you don't go out to kill a man you just go out to beat him. You went and you fought with him, you know, not because you had anything against him, you were just going for the money. And I'd say 99 times out of 100 you'd shake hands after the fight.

I could be working on the farm, then when it was Holbeck Shows or Feast, or Woodhouse, or Dewsbury Road I could come back, go round with the boys, my pals, get in the ring and have a go. When you got there to a showground, you'd try and make a bit of a fight up for two shilling, half-a-crown, ten shilling, a pound, whatever your pals could rake up they put on you. And you'd know if you lost, if you're going to lose, or if you thought you were going to lose there was no good fighting, you just went – I'm going to beat him and choose how hard you got hit you didn't feel it, it were the next day you felt it! When the bruises came out. You'd be sore next day like.

And up York Road, Shaftesbury, what they used to call the Shaftesbury picture house, there were boxing up there, and we used to follow it all up there you see. We used to go all over, Wakefield, anywhere there were shows; was any fighting, we'd be there. And as I say it wasn't because you thought you was a big man, you went for the bit of money. Well I've come out the ring unrecognisable to be honest with you. My mother's cried when she's seen me.

But I didn't lose, I never lost. It was just, I don't know, determination. I've seen me get it, put down, voices come, *"get up, they have nowt to eat"*, you'd get up and you'd get back in. If you thought you were tired you'd start saying, *"well I'm tired, you must be as tired as me, if not more tired."* And it'd give you more courage and you went in and you kept at it 'til that was the end of it.

Not doing the boxing never entered my mind. I mean today, lads that're boxing and love boxing, they've got more opportunities. They've got coaches and these clubs, they didn't have clubs when we was on the go. We had to go and find show grounds to fight. I mean Freddy Mills started on the show grounds, Tommy Farr started on the show grounds. I mean they didn't have a lot of chance in them days like they have today. If you get a lad with a bit of skill today, you'll get somebody to sponsor him.

In my day there were nothing like that, you see, and in my father's day it were worse still, it was harder. As I say, a young man can make a lot of money today doing it. They say it's a cruel sport. It isn't because there's more people gets injured and killed in other sports, like mountain climbing or these stuntmen, I know they buried a lad the other day, it were just one of them things. I mean every time you go out on the road with a van you can get killed, or with a car. You can be walking still get killed. But you don't think about getting killed.

And in the old days I can't ever remember anybody dying from fighting. Outside fighting is more vicious than what boxing is, because you've got a referee in a ring, outside you haven't. When you're doing the bare knuckle stuff there was no rounds, you just keep going. Everything goes, bar hitting a man below the belt, you don't do that. I mean, well, they'd shun you if you'd done a thing like that, it's a gentleman's fight.

LEE GAP FAIR 1955
Me and my family stopping on the Lee Gap Fair. These people are my relations and blood kin.

After my Dad died, I mean, I used to learn from old men, old-time fighters, you know, old dealing men and you could learn off of old men. Well dealing men was horsemen, they dealed in horses and you'd listen to him. You could learn off of him, you couldn't learn off a young boy, you learnt off old father, but with not having a father you used to cling to old men. And they'd tell you about the fights they had and all this kind of thing, you know.

All those old fairs, they've all died out. Appleby is still on the go and they've kept Lee Fair going, now they're trying to get Yarm Fair going. There isn't many things there, but they're trying to build it back up. Thorne Fair was a good fair because they always had a boxing booth and you could always get in and earn a few shillings there you see. But the fairs were mostly horses, it was all horses in them days.

Well I used to breed a lot of horses on Brown Lane. We'd breed them and run them on, while they were year-ons, two year olds, whatever age they was you'd sell them, as foals if a man come up, you see. I used to get men coming up, and I'd sell them to my pals. When you went to Yarm you didn't trail foals with you, you'd leave your foals behind in a field and take what could travel and then you'd deal on Lee Fair or at Yarm Fair, Appleby, Brough, Thorne you see.

There was odd women done it, well say the husbands had died, there was old, elderlish women, not young women, and they'd deal with the old men that they'd knowed all their life. They respected the woman you know and they didn't take advantage of her. They just had an ordinary deal, because she'd been fetched up with horses, and she knowed what she was talking about, and it might be one she'd bred, or two she'd bred, or one she'd bought off of someone, and she'd just deal the same as a man.

There's this new law out now that you can't travel. Not as I'm blaming anyone, they've put the blame on the 'new age' Travellers. Right, to me, I think that was an excuse to condemn it. I admit they were doing things that a Gypsy person wouldn't do. They were pulling over farmer's field, they'd maybe leave rubbish, I don't know. But I mean we would never have dreamt of pulling over farmer's fields not without doing work for them. We have been in his field, but we've had his permission because we've been working for him, but we'd never travel on a road, however dark it got, and think of pulling open a gate and pulling in, we'd find a roadside to pull over. But I think a lot of it's an excuse.

I mean it was bad enough for us, they'd maybe give us a night here and night there, then move us on. But we respected the law, we moved when we was told and we didn't leave any litter. If we was in a place, let's say we were lucky and we got into a place for two weeks, when we moved you couldn't have found a matchstalk. We'd even bury our ashes where we'd had an outside fire. We didn't just leave it piled there, or old tin cans. We dug a hole and we buried all our rubbish and put the grass sod back on. We'd cut the grass out like a square, dig a hole, put the earth back and the grass sod and that's how all the old Gypsy people used to do it. There was no litter left in our days.

APPLEBY FAIR 1996
Horse trading continues here in the traditional ways. It is still an important meeting place for all Gypsies and Travellers at the beginning of June each year.

Back then we travelled all over, right down to Cromer strawberry picking, we used to blackberry pick, apple pick and it was more like a working holiday, we made money and it was a change from being here all the time you see. I never went hop picking though. Years gone by they used to leave the houses and the farmers had sheds for them to sleep in and they used to have like a Gypsy fire outside. They'd leave all the pans and pots from one year and they were there when they went back. And they used to hop pick there. But I never did hop pick - strawberry picking, apple picking, all things like that, potato picking, sugar beet pulling, when I were younger like.

Tattie picking and all that, you know, very hard work that. Can you imagine going in a field where the leaves is white with frost and you've got to get at them with your bare hands? That's how you had to do it. I've seen men's fingers split right across with frostbite. You see you had to pull the beet in the winter. And if it were too frosty you had to leave them while they thawed out, before you could pull them. You didn't have a shovel or a spade. No, it was a sickle. You'd get them you know and pull them, feel the ends, take the tail of the root and then chuck off with the leaves and then you'd heap them. And when the block carts came, then you had to load them on. Men and women done it, yeah there wasn't many Travelling people, Gypsy people that didn't work on farms. They had to because there was no other way of making money, and as I say everybody couldn't go into a boxing ring to earn a pound. And I mean that's all you got was a pound.

When we was younger, up to me being twenty-one, we was never in the towns except for repairs; and a tyre-tightening on your caravan or your car or whatever, it was all in the country farm working.

Oh there's been a lot of changes. I mean when we was younger there wasn't such a thing as sites. The sites makes people depressed. I mean I feel sorry for the children, they get up of a morning, they go to school, which is a good thing, I mean I wouldn't like my grandchildren to grow up like me illiterate – I can't read nor write. But when they come out of that school, they come back to the caravan there's no parks for them to have little swings to play on. I mean when my grandchildren comes down here, *"come on grandad take me to the park"*, well, I've been that ill I couldn't do it, because I've had a bad do. When I could do, I used to take them down the park, and they used to enjoy themselves. I mean when they come out of school up on them sites there's nowhere for them to occupy little minds. They're just cooped up there waiting for next morning to go back into school, they're locked up all day, I know they have their little playtime in the school, but when they come back they've nothing to do, they get depressed.

Now anybody that tells me on them sites, that they're not depressed, I'd call them a liar to their face, because I know they're depressed. I've seen the changes in the people. I've seen their spirits die you know. They just give up because it's not the life they've been used to all their lives, they've been used to here and there.

I couldn't live in a house myself, I've knowed nowt else all my life, I'm happy as I am you know. I want to die outside. Putting me in a house is like putting a wild bird or a wild rabbit in a cage. It'll die. If you clipped a birds wings it'd still die. I don't know, you feel free, you know you feel free. I mean when we were young we was all over the place up to getting married like; Lincoln, Newark, Nottingham you know, Retford, all over the north of England, we were never still. As I say we had to keep moving. You could only work so long on a farm and then you'd go off again and whatever you could do for your living, you've done.

I mean we had nothing but believe me we was happy as kings. I've seen us wet through and trembling, and I've seen us hungry. We didn't cry with hunger, we was hungry, but we didn't cry. Because we know there were people in the world worse off than us, we was happy, we had peace of mind, we were free, we could go. We'd pull on a ground, they'd shift us, we'd shift, we didn't give them any aggro, we moved.

I've never been out of England in my life. I love my own country, I love England. Some as go abroad, I wouldn't want to go abroad, there's no country in the world as pretty as this, you've got greener grass here and greener trees than anywhere in the world, I think so. I mean that might just be me, I mean I love here. And I know they go to Spain and all that.

But then you're born to this climate, it shouldn't bother you, should it? I mean they go to Scotland, you don't get better scenery than what's in Scotland – it's beautiful. People go from this country, go abroad and they haven't seen their own country, you see. And I've heard the old people say I've been all over the world, when they was in the army, you know, there's no country like home. She's the prettiest piece of land on earth.

MY LOST PHOTOGRAPH WHICH WAS FOUND IN 1998

I was fifteen when this was taken, back in 1942. I got it took in Leeds at the corner of Briggate, it were near the 'Fifty shilling Taylors', where you could get a suit. Me and me cousin were going out and we got it took.

I'm wearing me Father's neckerchief. It was a silk one, a muffler, a chocolate dice one. All the Travellers wore them in them days.

I wore this one to remember me Dad and I had it for years. You never forget them if you've got something to look at.

The man that had this photo went blind and he gave it to me oldest son, Geordie, saying, 'I can't look at it no more and that's your Dad.'

He'd had that photograph for fifty-six years!

The Buxton Family

An old photograph of my Grandmother Mary Winters with her Dad Isaac.

Grandmother with her Mam and sister. This was taken in the 1920's.

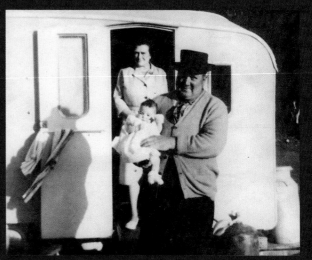

This shows me relatives with Henry Miller on Appleby Fair in the 1940's.

This is me Granny, Mary Winters and me Grandad Joe Buxton with me sister Julie in the New Forest in 1962.

...personal memories

We still go up to Appleby, every year. This photo was taken on our way back, at Brough where we had stopped for shopping.

We had just left Appleby in 1996 and were on our way to Smallways.

There is Arthur Gaskin in front of me and I'm stood with my Open Lot.

This wagon, which belongs to the family, was built by Philip Jowett in 1975 and then painted up by Yorkie Greenwood.

Eileen James

My name is Eileen James and I was born in Preston. I'm eighteen years old and married. My father, Lawrence Hanrahan, is from Ireland and my mother, Christine, is from England. I've got four brothers and four sisters. I'm the third oldest.

...telling her own story

When I was young we used to travel all over the country, everywhere: Oxford, Southend, Liverpool, all over. Moving to different places all the time, about every week. We moved because we had to, we'd get moved off by the Council. We used to travel with all different kinds of breed, different people, Connors and Dorans and McGinnleys. Me Daddy used to do tarmacing and rubbish jobs - clearing rubbish away from people's houses; tarmacing their drives, that's what they used to do.

When I was old enough I had to look after the small children. My bigger sister, she used to clean up and make the dinners, and my brother - he's older than me - he used to go out with me father working. When we got up in the morning we'd get washed and my sister would make our breakfast, we'd have our breakfast, then we'd play out all day.

Messing about, with what we'd find on the camp we'd make something of them. There wasn't really much, though. We weren't allowed to go off the camp, we had to stop around the trailers all day because moving to different areas all the time, there was different things going on you don't know about. You can't just walk off. We weren't allowed to go to the shops or anything like that. We had to stop there and do what we could on there.

When we came to a new place we'd pull on those lay-bys, where there's cafés. We'd pull on there and then the men would go around the town looking for a ground that they could pull on. And then when they'd find a ground - probably go for two or three hours looking for a ground - they'd come back again and they'd shift on it. Then we used to get about a week on, and then we'd be moved on.

Some areas, some towns, they'd let us stop for six weeks or longer, they'd let us stop as long as you want. It's got to be the middle of nowhere, though, around no houses and things like that. But when we used to move on next to houses, the people used to complain they didn't want Gypsies around their back garden.

We'd shift if, like, say me aunt was about 50 mile away in another town and we wanted to go and stop with her, we'd just shift. Other than that, the only way we'd move is if the Council moved us along. That's when we'd move. But sometimes, if we wanted to move ourselves and go, if things weren't working out proper, we'd go. Sometimes the people in the houses didn't want us to stay and they used to chuck stones and shout abusive language and all things like that. And me father and mother'd be frightened to go and leave us with my older sister in case of what they might do. So we wouldn't feel safe, so we'd have to move.

I went to school once in London for six weeks when I was nine, I never went for very long. It was because of the teacher, because this little boy in the classroom, he didn't like me, over being a Gypsy, so when it was time to go home, when everyone was out of the classroom, he stopped in and he took the teacher's pens out of her desk and he put them into my desk. And the next morning when we came back to school, the teacher was looking for a pen and she found it in my desk, so when I come into school she said to me *"What was these doing in here? Why did you take them?"* So I said *"I never."* But this other young girl, she was a nice young girl and she told me that the young boy done it, so I started arguing with the young boy, and the teacher blamed me for doing it because the young boy said he'd seen me doing it and we had a fight.

And then the next day all these teachers come to see me Mum and me Mum had to bring me back to the school to see the head teacher and I got expelled over it. And that was it, I never went to school again

but I've picked up some reading and writing. I don't know how, writing letters and that - trying to write letters. I don't know, the more I seemed to write, I seemed to learn more - more words and that. I know small words, but when it comes to big words I just can't do it.

It's worse for stopping today than what it was years ago. Travellers believe in living in trailers. Some Travellers won't even stop on a site, they don't believe in it - they believe in travelling around. The way they've been brought up - that's the way they want to stay. But it's getting very hard, this day and age, to stop anywhere. I think that's why there should be more sites made for people to go on.

I came to this site about five years back. We moved to this town, we stopped down Cross Green, and I don't know, the men just decided to pull up on a site, so we pulled on a site, and it would be going on five years, and I've been married two years. When we got married my father and mother shifted away, and we stopped on me mother-in-law's plot, and then we got our own.

COTTINGLEY SPRINGS LEEDS 1995
Me sister, Margaret, she'd come to stay with us. We were just going down the town and Donna took this photograph of us in front of the trailer.

The site's a lot different to the roadside. You've got your little shed and a toilet, and you get a bath whenever you want. You don't have to drive to garages for toilets, and you don't have to go to swimming baths to get a shower, 'cos when you're travelling you have to go to leisure centres to get a shower, and you have to drive off to use the toilet. It's very awkward. You have to get all your water from garages. And some people won't allow you to have it. Most garages will, but some, when you've been stopping in an area for so long, I think they can turn a bit queer at the garage, and they won't let you in. I don't know why, if it's being Travellers.

Some Travellers is bad, don't get me wrong, and some is good. Like people who lives in houses - some is good and some is bad. We're all people at the end of the day. Just because we travel around the country and we don't live in houses, they think we're different to them. I don't know why. People who lives in houses - I can get on really good with them. Mostly when you're travelling around the country and you pull into different areas, the people just don't want you there and that's it. I don't know why it is.

When big families travel around they will have maybe two or three trailers with different trailers for boys and girls. Like one is for the father and mother and the small children, and one'll be for all the boys and one for all the girls. But some people that haven't got very much money they can't afford a couple of trailers. They all have to stop in the one trailer but you only used the trailer for sleeping, you were all outside for the rest of the day.

Traveller parents are very strict on the girls, especially about boys and that. A few years back they wouldn't be allowed to talk to a boy, because they're frightened they'll run off. They're very strict on the girls. Don't allow them to have boyfriends, nothing like that.

The boys can do what they want, but girls can get a bad name, whereas boys can't. Boys can do what they want and walk away from it, but girls, if they go with a boy and do wrong, that's their name scandalised.

That's a very big thing in Travelling life, and if you get a bad name, you suffer the rest of your life.

HOLY FAMILY CHURCH, ARMLEY, LEEDS
This is me on my wedding day.
Everyone of us enjoyed ourselves. It was really nice.

With all Travellers, the only way you get out of it is if you move away and don't have nothing to do with Travellers. Just move away altogether. Move into a house or something. I wasn't allowed to do nothing.

When Travelling girls go with boys they have to do it behind their parents' back. And then the day they want to get married, the boy goes and asks for the girl and they'll say *"Yes you can marry"* and then they have a big do, get a wedding dress and all that. But when they say *"No"*, they end up running away and things get worse.

My mammy and daddy allowed me to get married. We had a proper wedding and everything with a lot of people there. Oh it was lovely, to tell you the truth. It was really nice. Everyone was lovely. I had five bridesmaids and one pageboy. My sister was my bridesmaid and me husband's brother was the best man.

I got married in Leeds and I still haven't moved out of Leeds since. We were supposed to have shifted this summer but things aren't going proper, so we never moved away.

When you're used to travelling all your life, it's funny when you don't. If you stay in the one place, it does your head in. It's very depressing. I've never in my life stopped so long in a place and never moved for five year. I've never stayed in a place five year in me life. It can get to you a lot, especially as my family don't live here, I don't get to see any of my own people. It can get on me nerves some times. So that's why I have to clean up every day and keep me mind occupied. 'Cos when I think, I get very, very depressed. I don't like it.

It's very important to keep your trailer clean but when you're travelling it can be very awkward to keep your place clean. Sometimes you haven't got enough water to use on your cleaning, and you need water for making tea and drinking. Two cans of water doesn't go very far. And it's getting the water, because they won't let you have it. So you learn to use maybe one dish of water to clean your trailer - you'll wipe all around first, and then do your floor with it. I clean my trailer every day.

When I get up - on here - I get washed and make some tea and get my breakfast, and then I wash up after that, then I make more tea then I clean all up, and then I do my slab and clean my shed and feed the dogs and that. It takes up all my time.

They could do a lot of things to improve the site. They could try and put postboxes on the wall to get your own mail, 'cos people's getting all my mail. The problem with the mail is, when the postman comes he gives it to anyone, and there's people opening letters and going through your private things what you don't want people to know about. And that's why we could do with our own postbox with our own number on it, so the postman can get out of his motor and put it in. Then I can go and get me own mail out of me box. There's not one person gets their own mail on here, everyone else gets the mail for them.

And the other thing is we could do with some new fencing because when I come on here there was no fencing, it was all open. And I had to go and I had to find them boards and I had to nail them up meself. No fencing means that people are coming in, in and out of your slab, kicking footballs and banging outside your trailer, dogs coming on, messing on the ground. That's why I had to put them boards up meself. I had no choice but to put them up. Because people just run in and out, taking things when you're not there, going into your shed and taking things. There's a few times things have been took out of me

shed. They've punched me doors through, then kicked it, broke the lock. When I first come on I was on me own about three week, and the shed was rough but I had all my things in it, some washables, bedspreads and things like that got took out.

We get the trailers made in a place in York, they call it Romanes Caravans. They're different to caravans that house people have, there's no sinks in them or toilets. We don't need sinks, we don't believe in needing sinks, we just use a bowl. We don't believe in having a toilet in the caravan. You can get them put in, if you want, when you're getting the caravan made, but we don't use them. We've never used them.

Travellers decorate the trailer with washables on the floor, with bedspreads, some nice photo frames up and a set on the kitchen - a set of pots like. But they all have different kinds of sets. All they usually have is a nice set in the kitchen and a bedspread and washables down. Probably a vase of flowers or a lamp. The old people used to collect the Crown Derby china but the young people, they won't have it up, we don't like it, I go for little modern things. It takes a long time keeping all the glass and chrome clean, especially formica, you have to look after it.

The chrome trailers and the ones with colours on are all in the past. They've gone plainer now, when you get a new trailer now they're all plain white. New trailers start at about £13,000. So most people will not buy new but will buy off Travellers. If I wanted that trailer out there, I'd go out and ask him to sell it, and he'd sell it if he was getting the right money, he'd sell it, no matter what.

ADA'S ANNIVERSARY 1997
Me with my son, Danny, with Lena and Violet. It was taken in the 'Wagon and Horses', Holbeck.

When you're young and starting off, it's very hard. We get lots of things for wedding presents when we get married. From uncles and grannies and grandads, and what they leave us when they die. What they've got is shared out between all the grandchildren. That's how we get the trailer and what we've got.

I can't say whether we'll stop on the site because you don't know, anything can happen. We could just move, we could move tomorrow. You don't know these things but we'll never go into a house. Never.

Travellers will never stop travelling. Never. Even when they're really old, they won't go into a house. They have these elderly homes, don't they, where people go to - well, Travelling people when they get old, don't go to places like that. They wouldn't leave their family to go into a place like that. They don't believe in it. They believe in stopping at home until they die, and then they get buried. They won't go into old people homes I think they'd die quicker if they went anywhere like that. They get looked after with their own. When they get bad and when they get old, all the family comes and stops with them and looks after them until they die.

If they're in hospital when they die, they get took out and brung home and the whole place gets - nothing but white sheets get put up - and a big cross, and candles lit, and there's only one or two persons allowed in to see the person, because you're not allowed a lot of body heat, and then they wake them for two days. They sit up - don't go to sleep. They sit up all night, making tea and sandwiches. And they 'wake' the person.

All the family comes from everywhere - everyone comes. There'll be thousands and thousands. There've been a lot of wakes held on this site. And a lot of people comes. Usually every Travelling person who dies has been in the newspaper because it's been that big a funeral. It's been in the newspapers, it's been on telly because when they go into the graveyard, there's that many people, driving the motors, they can't get nowhere, there's that many people.

For twelve months after the person's died they wear black. Not the children, just the big people like, not everyone - just the family, and the sisters and brothers, and the eldest daughters and sons. Some people don't come out of black ever, don't believe in wearing nothing only black clothes. They don't believe in having Christmas, they won't get married. If someone died today and say this young girl was supposed to get married tomorrow, the wedding would be called off. They'd have to wait for twelve months after, 'til the person's gone to heaven and that. Then they get married, but they can't get married straight away. And they don't believe in going to dances, they don't believe in going nowhere for twelve months. They sit down at home for twelve months.

Religion is important, I got christened, had me Holy Communion, had me Confirmation. You have to have all that when you're a Catholic. If you haven't had it done, you have to have it done before you get married. A nun comes out before you take your Holy Communion, probably once a week to talk to you about it and explains everything to you and then you go and have it done. When I had me Holy Communion I had a dress, but when I had me Confirmation I had a suit on. All the family came, it's a big thing, really.

I meet up with family at christenings and weddings; if any of me aunts, any of me uncles, any of me cousins, any of me relations is having their child christened or getting married or funerals - anything - we're always there. That's the only way we meet up, like weddings, things like that.

I'm only having two children. Years ago Travelling people used to have fourteen or fifteen children, but not any more. They're just stopping it all now, they're not having big families. In a few years to come you won't hear tell of people having big families. My child will know the English and Irish language, Gaelic. English Travellers speak different to Irish Travellers. But my child will know English Romanes and Irish Gaelic. I'll definitely send my child to school.

I'll give my child what I never had and make sure it knows how to read and write and knows everything. 'Cos it's bad when you don't know how to read and write; it's an awful thing. It's made it very difficult for me. When you have to sign papers, you don't know what you're signing. You just sign them. You could be signing your life away, you don't know the difference.

But I'll make sure, definitely, my children knows everything. They'll go to school and have more than I ever had. With travelling so much - one town for a week and then another town - we just never went to school. If I'm on a site (I can't see me being travelling) but if I'm on a site when I have my child and it's time to go to school, it will go to school. I'll make sure it knows how to read and write and knows how to get a job, and things like that, things that you should know.

ON COTTINGLEY 'A' SITE, LEEDS
This is me and Danny with our son, Danny, riding the horse. This was taken last year and Bennie is with us holding the other horse.

The Stewart Family

WAGONS IN IRELAND

I got this photograph from my son, who got it from an old Scotch man in London. The Scotchman said that he'd been all over the world and had always mixed with Travellers. He wanted to give this photo to a person who carried the name 'Stewart', because he knew that '...these are the people on the photograph'.

My son got the photo for me because I am a Stewart and I know that these are all my relations.

This was taken in County Armagh, Ireland, in 1914.

The two American actors in the centre, in suits, gathered up all the Travellers to have their photograph taken with them. The Travellers are going to a Fair, horse dealing and selling the flowers they had made. All these people are genuine Gypsy people, through and through.

These are my parents, cousins and second cousins, the Stewarts, the Whites, the Williamsons and also, the McCallisters.

The wagons are 'Reading' wagons and one belonged to the Williamson family and the other was my Great Grand Uncle's.

Maggie Jones

...meeting the famous

The Stewart Family

Me Father, Jimmy Stewart, put the top on this lorry when we were children in Ireland. The big wagon is behind. I was born in a wagon and we travelled all over Great Britain - England, Ireland, Scotland and Wales.
This was taken in County Tyrone in 1935.

This shows the barrel top wagons we had in the early 30's with all the family. Me Grandfather, Big Jock White - he was in the army for years, is sat in the middle. Me Dad, Jimmy, and Mam, Nancy, are on the left.

...times long past

JOHN STEWART'S RECOLLECTIONS

STAFFORDSHIRE, 1954
This is me and two friends, Mary Burnside and Mary Price when we were stoppin' in Staffordshire.

STAFFORDSHIRE, 1956
This is old Jimmy Stewart, me Dad, with Lady his granddaughter. It was taken in me sister Mary's trailer when we were all stoppin' in Winsbury.

DERBY IN THE FIFTIES
This is me Dad, Jimmy Stewart with me sister, Katy and Duck Ward, a pal of hers. We were all stoppin' together right in the middle of Derby.

This is on the Town Moor at Newcastle, in 1957. There's me, with me cousin, Billy Gentle and his Dad, Roy Gentle, Paddy Maughan, Joe Lowther and Paddy Harker. We were all up for the Fair, stoppin' in a big field together. It was beautiful in those days, you could just get up and go on and walk down the Fair and everything was the same as you left it when you got back.

The Stewart Family

SCOTLAND, 1960

This was at a gala day in Scotland. They used to 'Toss the Caber' and 'Throw the Stones' and they'd have parades all 'round the town and in the villages.

There's Me and May, with my two brothers, Jimmy and Alec and our two children, Jack and Dolly.

We were stoppin' in some yards with the trailers. It was my uncle's place in a village called 'Fallhouse', near Coatbridge.

This was taken in the square of this little town.

NEWCASTLE, IN THE EARLY SIXTIES

This is me brother, Jimmy, on Newcastle Town Moor with the children, Dolly and Lucy and Jack riding Jock the stallion.

LONDON, 1968

This is when we were down in London, on Petticoat Lane, with Nancy and Boy.

...in times gone by

This is me and Nancy and the twins on Slackley Lane Common, Birmingham, in 1972.

This is me, T.J. and John with Dolly and friends, camping in 1994.

The Stewart Family

This is me Great Grandfather, Walter Lee, with Olivine, Andy, Eileen and Rose, my Grandmother. You can see their horse-drawn wagon and cooking irons.

This was taken in 1926 in Camarthen, Wales.

This is Lena Gray and her family in 1952. She is my Great-Grandmother.

This is Lena, years ago, stopping in Ireland.

...just thinking back

TRACEY STEWART'S RECOLLECTIONS

Lena cooking outside on the open fire.

This is me, Tracey Brazil, standing in the trailer doorway before I married Boy. I'm with me Mam, Pam, and sisters and friends.

Tilly Kelby

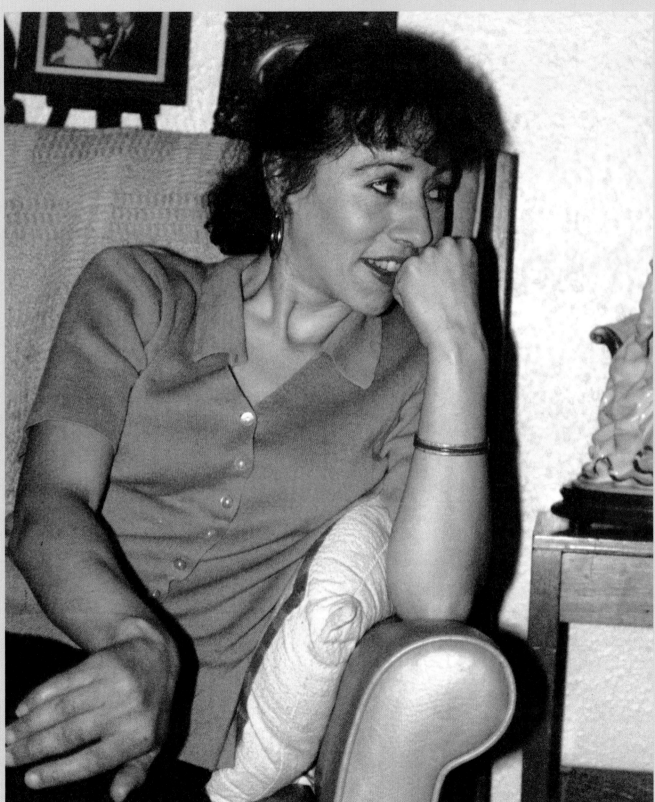

My name is Tilly Kelby and I'm twenty-eight years old. I was born in Salford in Manchester. I'd see myself as an Irish Traveller although I've never been in Ireland. I've lived in England all my life but both my parents were born in Ireland, so I class meself as Irish.

...in her own words

All my brothers and sisters are the same as me; they were all born in England but they class themselves as Irish as well. They've all got a nickname. I've got a nickname as well. My name is Michelle, they call me Tilly. I wouldn't really answer for Michelle - I'm used to being called Tilly.

When I was young we lived in a trailer and we travelled around from camp to camp. We spent more time around Yorkshire than we did in Manchester. We moved back up to Manchester when I was about fourteen and we stayed there on and off for about three years. We'd pull back down to Leeds or Bradford for a couple of weeks then we'd go back up to Manchester. But mostly my memories of being a child is down around Yorkshire. We'd camp mostly on waste ground and crofts where houses had been knocked down. We stopped mostly with family, me uncles and aunts, and when I was smaller me grandparents. We didn't really stay with big crowds when I was a child, just a few, mostly people we knew well.

When I got older we stayed with crowds of people but it was mostly five to six trailers when I was little. I remember we stayed on one ground - Low Moor they called it - and we were on there for years. When we first came on it was our own family - me father and mother and brothers and sisters, and me grandfather and grandmother, and a few of me uncles and aunts. And if a trailer pulled in, they wouldn't stay very long, they'd pull in and then they'd pull out again.

When we were on the camps there'd be a group of us children who'd play together and go wandering. Just play and do normal things, like every child does, we'd get into our fair share of mischief, but children do, don't they? Then, when I was about eight we pulled into Batley, behind a big pub - they used to call it the Showboat and there were a few more trailers on, but it was still like just mostly our own family, and that was the first time that I went to school. The School Board came down and made us all go to school.

School was terrible, it was awful, because when we got to the school the children knew we were Travellers so they started teasing us and calling names. Don't get me wrong, we'd give as good as what we got, better as a matter of fact. I remember I beat the school bully - I pulled a bookcase down on top of him because he was bullying me, I nearly squashed him.

The school teacher sent us in to the library, it was in the middle of the class - it was two bookcases put together. You got in behind it to get the books out and she sent us in to tidy it up, me and the school bully, 'cos she knew we weren't getting on. So she must have thought if she sent us in to do something together, we might get on a bit. But he used to whisper abuse to me like *"Gypsy"* and *"Smelly Gypsy"* and nasty things.

I got really fed up, I really got sick of it and he was whispering to me so that the schoolteacher couldn't hear. So I grabbed hold of the edge of the bookcase and I pulled it right down on top of him and his legs were sticking out and he was kicking underneath this bookcase, and his full body it was, with all these books on. So I said to him *"Now you'll leave me alone, won't you?"*, and he did leave me alone. He never said another word from that day to this. He was terrified of me after that; honestly he was. It all stopped.

This shows me granny Esther, on the left, when she was a young woman.

Her brother Jimmy Wilson is sat in the middle.

They're just goin out durrekin' and hawkin' for their living.

We were nasty though. The way they were to you, they were nasty to you, so you had to be the same way. There was no such a thing as going to a school and making friends with them. It was always there what you were, you were a Gypsy, a dirty Gypsy. You felt like you had to be really tough and act really hard and tough with them.

You know how children go to school and make friends with children, well we could never do that, it was always a battle between us. I was only at school about four weeks, and then we were leaving, so that was it. We went about four weeks and we got into a lot of bother. There wasn't a day that didn't go by, 'cos they don't do it any more now - beat the children with the cane - but when we were going to school they used to beat you with a pump over the hand and there wasn't one day we weren't marched up to the headmaster and whacked with his shoe over the hand. It wouldn't be for nothing - it would be for doing harm. It'd be for taking some of the children's things, or it'd be mischief. We were always causing some kind of mischief.

On the camps the smaller children didn't have jobs to do but the older ones, as they got older did. When you were say five, six, seven, eight, you didn't. All day you just played and wandered and carried on and as you got a bit older you got jobs. Maybe the girls washed dishes and the floor, and maybe made tea. And as you got that bit older you'd have to take over and clean out the trailer, and maybe even cook. The boys'd go out with their fathers.

The best times on the camps, really, was in summer time. You'd be stopping on a nice field, nice green grass, and there'd be plenty of company, maybe your own cousins or relations, people you got on with. They were the best times because everybody would get outside and they'd maybe light a big fire and all the grown ups'd get around and chat. All the children would be listening on, running around and playing. When we were small and we were around camp you seemed to be always happy. Everybody shared, whatever they had. If you were short of something, if all the men was gone off, and the women was just on the camp with the children, and they were short of bread before they got to a shop, or water, they'd share, they'd share with everybody. It was a different life, it was more sociable. When you were travelling, say there was five or six families travelling together, it was just like one big happy family. All my happy memories is when I was a child because it is really different now.

UNCLE, AUNT AND FATHER

The youngest is my father Chickie when he was two.

My aunt Queenie was four and Ben, sitting on the horse, was three.

It was taken in 1934.

At that time, when I was small, most Travelling people used to go and look for scrap, gather scrap, or things like that. And then as the years went on, most Irish people went onto tarmacking, rubbish jobs and things, but it was mainly scrap iron then, so the boys just used to go out with their fathers.

They'd mostly just go round hawking the houses for scrap. If they came across a yard where there was a bit of scrap metal, they'd go in about it, but it was mainly houses. They'd get the scrap down the back of the houses, they'd have scrap thrown around that could have been there for years and someone'd come along and ask for it. There was always a bit of scrap lying around, not like now.

The women worked as hard as the men, plus they had to mind the children and feed them, shop and do all that as well. Women brought up the family and they helped the husband gathering the scrap.

MANCHESTER 1960
Me Mammy and Daddy were staying in a house in Manchester.
Our Joe was just a new baby then.

Me dad gathered scrap. He used to gather old rags too, he put bills in the doors asking for it. Then he'd take it to - well they always called it the rag stores. They used to take it to this big mill place, where they recycled the clothes and sell the rags in weight, they just baled them up.

I remember he used to have lorry loads of rags, they'd be piled up really, really, high and when they'd come back you used to have to sort them out, you'd have to sort the woollens out, you'd get more money for the woollens.

And if they were wet, I remember, you used to have to dry them out because most stores wouldn't have the rags if they were wet. You'd cover them up, and if it was a dry day they'd just leave back the cover and leave them to dry out.

So Travellers have been recycling stuff for a long time, they were always environmentally friendly!

The happiest days of our lives were being on the waste grounds. Now in Leeds you might get stopping for a week or two, maybe, here and there, if there's not a big crowd of you and you keep quiet and all round your trailers tidy. But long term staying like you used to get years ago, three or four months, maybe more sometimes, you won't get that any more.

Now nearly all the places where we stayed, there's all buildings on them, and has been for years, so there's not really many places where people can pull in now around Leeds or Bradford or Batley. The only place, really, is the sites.

People have moved onto the sites because they've been forced onto them against their will. There's hardly nobody travelling around this part now. Most of the Travelling people around Leeds and Bradford is in the sites - there's two sites in Bradford - so there's no travelling up and down, really.

Water was never a problem on the camps. Anyone would give you a can of water and you always managed that way. It's more of a problem now if you move off the site. You used to get water out of the garage, we used to use the big aluminium churn cans. But when we were small if the men were going out hawking and you run out of water we used to have chrome 'jack cans' they used to call them. So if me Daddy or anyone wasn't there to go for the water and you had none you'd just walk across to a house with a pram. Anyone would give you a small can of water. But we used to mainly get cans of water out of the garages. Most times we didn't have to pay for it but an odd person would be awkward and maybe charge you fifty pence for a can.

Heating was never a problem, we had a stove inside the trailer. As a matter of fact, it's more of a problem now than it was then because when we were children we were used to that life. You were used to getting up in the morning and it being a bit nippy before the fire was lit. You were used to sometimes going a couple of hours without water, 'til someone came back from fetching it. You were used to getting a big dish of water and having a wash in the trailer. We were always clean. You were always warm. You were always well fed. It was never a problem. Heating's more of a problem now because it's very hard to keep the electric going, you know the electric fires are so expensive. When I was a child coal was cheap and you'd always have a big red fire going. You could even go over a field sometimes and find the coal, you could pick it.

The women didn't go out to work they mostly stayed at home, cleaned up and looked after the children. An odd one would go out to the houses, with the charms, 'the swag' as they called it. They used to go out with pegs and needles and things. Maybe a couple of women would go out together and it would really just be to see if they could beg a few nice clothes for the children. 'Cos not many women bought new clothes then for the children. They were all begged. What come out of the rags and what they begged out of the houses. Well that's all that went on us and I was very happy with 'em.

There was no such a thing, you know, when we were little, about fashion. You know how children five and six year old now and they won't wear clothes unless they're in the fashion? I didn't even know what the fashion was, to tell you the truth. It didn't bother me. If I got a new pair of socks or a new bit of ribbon, of a Saturday when me Mammy would go to the shops, I'd think it was lovely. Me mammy used to make clothes when we were smaller. She used to make dresses for us, she knitted blankets for the beds and I remember she used to make trousers for me Daddy.

We'd be mainly shifted off a camp, we didn't move 'cos we wanted to. We were mainly evicted. You could be six months, sometimes you could be twelve months on a camp before you were moved. Now you're two or three days, maybe a week. But you wouldn't go very far, you'd just maybe go a couple of miles down the road. We were nearly three years down Domestic Street and we were two or three years on Lower Moor. This was going back before my Father died, and he'll be eleven years dead, in June.

Going back before he died it wasn't as bad for shifting but don't get me wrong there was more prejudice. The prejudice against Travellers now isn't as bad - that's one thing that has got better. They have more understanding for Travellers. But in regard of Travellers getting staying around places you don't get as long but I think that's because there's so many sites now.

MANCHESTER 1970

We were stopping in some old lane in Manchester when I was small and I'm with me Daddy.

Well, when I was a child I never had no contact with *"country people"*. I still say *"country people"*, no disrespect, it's just a name, it's just like us being called *"Travellers"*. Country people are people that live in houses and was born and bred in houses. When I was a child, we never had no contact with anyone like that. The first contact that I ever can remember having with anyone from a house was the first time I went to school. Before that the most contact I had was going into a shop but I never sat down and spoke with anyone. Even though we were camping in a town, sometimes in the dead centre of the town we never had any contact. We lived in a world of our own really, just with our own people.

I think that's good that that's changed because we are only people after all, we're all the same. The only way you can realise that they're not all prejudiced is to have contact with them, and speak to them, and then you realise that they are individuals, that they are no different. There is still a lot of prejudice but there's not as much now. When I was a child you couldn't walk down the street without somebody calling you *"Gypsy"*. And they seemed to know what you were. No matter what, they seemed to know you were a Gypsy.

There are differences in the culture and the beliefs and in the way we live. Well me brother's married to someone who was brought up in a house, a girl from Leeds and he lives in a house. More boys seem to marry out than girls. You only hear of a very very odd Travelling girl marrying out but I know an awful lot of men that are married outside. I think it's because Travelling people have got their own ways. I know we do look the same, but we have got an awful lot of differences. Travellers are more strict. Travelling girls worry more, I think, about their reputation, of what people will say. If a Travelling girl was found to be going with an outsider, well that would be a scandal. It would be alright for a Travelling girl to go out if she went with other girls, providing her father knew the girls, knew their people, knew what they were like. Then it was alright, she could go. Travellers are very strict about their daughters. The older generation of Travelling people, they're even more strict. It has to be something really outrageous before the younger generation will talk about it but it doesn't have to be very much for the older generation because some of them are really ridiculously strict.

Probably because when they were younger they weren't allowed to wear a skirt above their ankles. Years ago, young Travelling girls weren't even allowed to wear lipstick, if you wore lipstick you weren't very nice, or if you wore a skirt above your ankles or even nail varnish. Single Travelling girls will go out now, to a night club or a pub or a disco and they'll have a drink which I don't see anything really wrong with, if they don't do any harm, then fair enough. But years ago, or even now, with the older generation, that was just unheard of. You weren't a very nice girl to be doing that.

I don't know what it is, but in some ways Travelling people are more like Asian people about their daughters. Like Asian people, Travellers more or less years ago picked the husbands for their daughters. If they liked the boy and they liked his people and he was a 'decent enough boy', as we would say, then it was alright, it was fine. Go ahead, by all means. But if they were any kind of bad people, troublesome, or anything like that, then no. In that case, then, a girl would run away. They'd just run away and get married.

So there are lots of differences. We live different. We have our own way of speaking. We dress the same but you can pick a Traveller out, even if they were boiled in a pot. Put 'em into a pot of stew and boil 'em and pick 'em out and put 'em in a crowd and you can tell your own. You can tell 'em a mile away. I can walk down a street and see maybe two Travelling girls and maybe twenty young gorgio (non-Traveller) girls, and you can pick out the two Travelling girls.

I remember one day, I went into a shop in town and I was looking around. The man didn't bother, he didn't even give me a second look when I walked in, until I started speaking. I said something to my niece and as soon as he heard me speaking he looked at me and he wanted me out of the shop - he couldn't wait to get me out of the shop, because he knew what I was. When he heard me speaking he said he was closing the shop. I thought it was funny but I didn't say anything.

So I walked out and stood in an archway next door to the shop and I said to me Mammy *"I'm waiting to see if he really is closing that shop."* So I waited and he didn't close the shop, I was watching people going in. So I went back in and then I really did get angry. I said *"You're closing the shop, are yer? You told me a minute ago you were closing the shop".* I said *"You know what you are? You are racist. The only reason you said you were closing the shop was when you heard me speaking, you knew I was a Traveller".* I said *"I don't steal but if I were going to steal I would find something better than what you've got in here, because all you've got in here is a load of junk. You haven't got anything in here that I'd want to buy anyway. But I just came in here for curiosity, to have a look".* And I walked out again. But it really hurt me, that he could be so bad-minded. I've had that a lot, it used to hurt me, but now it doesn't bother me.

I remember one time, we were staying in Manchester, in Salford and we were staying on a croft, they call it, a big piece of waste ground, and the police came. First of all they started taking off the tops of the generators and they were chucking dirt down in the petrol tanks and then they started taking off the tops of the cans and emptying out all the water. They used to persecute us. If they wanted to shift yer, they'd come at the worst time they could. They'd come at about six o'clock in the morning, when you'd be in bed, or ten or eleven o'clock at night, of a cold night or a cold morning to shift yer. You're very vulnerable in a trailer, the minute something hits one of 'em, God forbid. If you put something straight through the window and hit a child when they're sleeping.

Have you ever noticed on a camp how Travellers go around, have you ever seen Cowboys and Indians how they goes in a circle, well Travellers do that? That's why they do that, they put the trailers in a circle. 'Cos you are vulnerable. And the motors stay in a large circle round the trailers for safety. You've got to know where to put your trailer, so that you are sort of protected. You can't just put it anywhere. The ones for small children are put in a circle in the middle.

You'll very rarely put your trailer near houses or near a bank or near a tree, 'cos it's dangerous. It's got to be out in the open where you can watch around. At night time you are a bit frightened when you're sleeping in your beds because you are very vulnerable.

When I was a little girl Travellers used to like Crown Derby, lots of cut glass - they used to have cut glass baskets and the bowls and the vases. And they loved cushions - lace cushions and cushions with bows and all these kind of things but now that's all gone out. They like their homes plain, with just a few bits and pieces up and down but Travelling people does still like colourful and fancy things, they love lace cushions. They go for colours and they do like things like that but their taste has changed a bit - they haven't got the same taste as they used to have.

You can tell someone's doing well by the things they have: their trailers and their motors. They'll put their money mostly in their trailers and their motors. They usually go and get the trailers made but the trailers Travellers have, again that's changed. They go more now for touring trailers, smaller, holiday sort of trailers. Where years ago it used to be the big trailers, with plenty of chrome and beading with Formica inside and stoves, they don't bother with chrome now, they've got a lot plainer.

Most of them doesn't even buy big trailers because the people that is travelling around, even if they are on sites and want to come off for a couple of months it's not as easy to tow a bigger trailer around. I think it's changed because the Travellers' lifestyle's changed because years ago they'd stick to the one area and maybe you'd get a couple of months on a ground. Now you pull on a ground and you could have to be off tomorrow. Well, to lift a big heavy trailer, full of chrome and full of Formica and put it onto a tow bar is not an easy thing, and to do that every second or third day is very hard. Whereas if they've got a small touring trailer it's easier, they just hook it up and they're gone.

When you have to pack to leave you have to take down everything breakable - your ornaments, your cups, your dishes, your television whatever. Make sure it's all safe because when the trailer's moving you've got to make sure nothing's going to be broke. It's a wonder too, because all the shifting about we used to do, that nothing ever really did get broke but if something did get broke it would be your fault because you hadn't packed it down safe enough. You'd get your quilts, your blankets, your pillows and you'd take down your television and just pack a few pillows, something soft around it so that it wouldn't

move. You'd wrap your dishes in towels, clothes, whatever you could find, and just sit them down on top of each other, all in one big pile on the floor. Because you were that used to it, you knew what way to pack things, what way they were safe. Even now, you're used to it, you know what way to pack them down, you don't pack them in cupboards or boxes or anywhere. And you do it quick as well, everything I have in this trailer now, I could pack 'em all down, maybe in a matter of five or ten minutes.

There was no time. When me Dad or any of the men was ready to shift, you'd got to be ready in minutes, they don't give you an hour or two hours and you have to have everything down and it's your job to make sure everything's safe so it won't get broke. Well it's mostly the men who decide when you shift or the Council or the police even. But it was mostly the Council 'cos the men was glad to get staying if they were working. They'd stay there and be grateful to get staying on a ground no matter what it was like.

LEEDS 1987
Our Queenie and me Mammy when they were stopping in Belle Isle.

Any trailer is always for sale. Even now there's no such thing as a trailer that's not for sale. If one man offers another man enough money. Even though they were your homes, if a man came down and named a good price, well you had to take your things out and that was it - it was sold. I've even known Travellers to sell trailers when they've got them made, the trailers hadn't even been took out of the place where it's been made and they've selled them. As long as one man is offering another man enough money, they were for sale and still are. Travellers are still the same way.

Most Travelling people would never really get sick of looking at their trailer because the longest they would have one, maybe, would be six months - maybe not even that.

I think the ear piercing, I don't know, it's like tradition. Every little girl in a family had their ears pierced, it was, still is, mostly little girls. Travellers'll buy a little boy a ring or a chain for his neck but mostly you'll see a little girl covered in jewellery. I was only about three days old when I had my ears pierced. My uncle pierced my ears, with a needle and a bar of soap. Me sister, she was the same. And then when your ears have healed up a little bit, a big pair of earrings was stuffed in your ears, and that was it really. You'll hardly see a little Travelling girl without a pair of earrings in her ears.

And the Travelling people used to be very big on sovereigns: sovereign rings, sovereign chains. They like a lot of jewellery. But that's changed as well, you don't really see that as much now. You'll see a woman with a pair of earrings in her ears, or a ring, but they don't really wear them now unless they're going anywhere. You don't really see as much jewellery any more, it's only the odd one, or maybe an older Travelling woman with all the jewellery. But not the young women.

I don't really think it was a sign of showing their wealth because I've known a lot of poor people, I still do know a lot of poor people, older people, and they're covered in jewellery. I think Travellers liked that sort of thing and that was it, a lot of them didn't wear all them things just to say that they had money. I can't really explain it, but it's just a thing with Travellers.

I came to this site about five year ago give or take a couple of month. Before that we were just travelling around on the grounds in Leeds. We were on the top site first but we didn't have a plot there, we were just staying with my sister and her family. And we were still pulling off and travelling around the grounds. We were on the top site for about twelve months on and off. We'd go off for a couple of months or a week or so and come back again. Then my sister got a plot on here and we just decided we'd pull up for a while. We pulled onto this plot and then we never left. They gave us a plot, worse luck, and we never left.

I really do think that the travelling days are finished now, but for Travelling people it will always be in their blood. It's like a bird being caged up. Even me, meself, when the warm weather comes on - even in the winter sometimes - I can't explain it, unless you feel it yourself. The best way I can explain it is it's like a hunger - you get a hunger - a longing comes over you, and you just want to be away, you want to be on the roads, just want to go somewhere.

Even now when we've been on here five year, a longing comes over you and you just want to go. We haven't been off for quite a while now. We might go away this summer for a little while. I don't even mind if it's only for a couple of weeks, just a little break. But even though I don't really like this place, once you've been on a site and once you've been settled down, you're never the same, you just can't cope on the road the same because you do miss the things that you have on the site. You miss the water, you miss having a bath you miss things like that. You don't feel it is difficult until you've had them things. Don't get me wrong, you do manage. I'd manage better than someone that was never on the road and after a couple of weeks it probably wouldn't bother me but for the first couple of weeks of being back on the road I do find it hard. The hardest thing is washing after being used to a bath on the site.

The main problem with this site is they made it too big and they put too many people on it. My ideal site would be for about eight or nine families. To hand pick the families that get on with each other because if you don't get on with your neighbours it doesn't make a very pleasant living environment, does it?

But we're even closer than people living in houses. Because when your neighbour goes inside and closes his door, you're not looking at him all day, you don't see him no more till he comes out of his house again but on here you're looking at your neighbours and they're looking at you - they're watching everything you're doing. They know everything you're doing and you know everything they're doing and if you don't get on with those people, it doesn't make a very pleasant living environment. And most people on here doesn't get on with each other. And I don't really think that's a very pleasant place to live.

So my ideal idea of a site would be to hand pick the families - families that gets on with each other. I'm not saying there wouldn't be any arguments still because we're all human - everybody falls out now and again, but if it's the right kind of people, you can work out your differences.

Plus if it was only a few and they'd known each other well, and they got on with each other, then if one lot of them was making a mess and breaking anything on the site, you could sort it out civilly. Where this site is constantly like a pigsty. They're breaking this and they're emptying rubbish here and doing this and doing that and you can't say anything about it. You've just got to put up and shut up and just live with it, and that's it. So you're living in a pigsty and you're living with people who hate yer. So it's not a very happy environment.

My hopes for the future, they are only hopes to be honest with yer, I can't see them happening or coming to much, are that they find somewhere else for us to go - to separate the people on here, break them up into smaller groups and put them on different places, and knock this site completely - knock it down and start afresh. That's what I would like to see happen. Honestly, break this down and make it into two separate sites.

CAMPS IN LEEDS

OVERNIGHT CAMP IN LEEDS IN THE THIRTIES

This is me Aunt Lucy and Uncle Tommy Gaskin cooking their dinners on a camp fire. You can see the old black pan on the kettle iron.

Tommy was a wagon painter and builder. He's got an old Bill Wright's wagon and the other one is just home made.

You can see the chrome can and the old Tiller mantle on the front of the wagon.

They were stopping overnight in Leeds as they were travelling through.

Mary Lowther

1930's

CAMPS IN LEEDS

HORSE DRAWN WAGONS TRAVELLING IN LEEDS IN THE FORTIES

We travelled like this all our lives, two or three families together with the wagons and horses and the flat cart at the back. We travelled mostly with me uncle Fred's family. It was a really close community then.

We worked more on the land and life was hard.

These wagons were on the Leeds to Selby road, travelling from one camp to the next.

Righteous Price

1940's

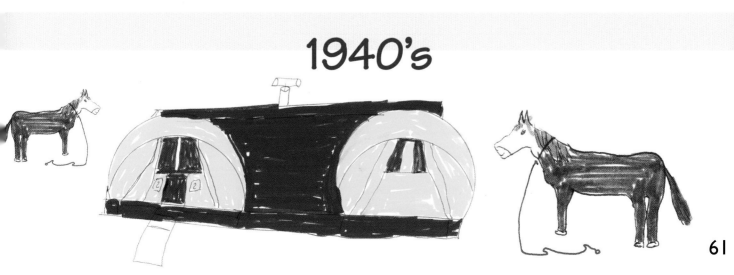

WAITING FOR LEE GAP FAIR 1955

We were all stoppin' on Bagnall Green in Woodkirk, Leeds. We were waiting for the Fair at Lee Gap in 1955. There's me brother with me and all the children around the campfire, with all our friends and relations.

Bob James

1950's

CAMPS IN LEEDS

GYPSY FAMILIES STOPPING IN BIRKBY BROW WOOD 1959

This was a traditional stopping place, at Howden Clough End, Morley in Leeds on 12th March 1959.

Isaac Nicholson, his brother, Towie, and Tot Ewebank from Doggie. They used to stop there regular when they were visiting Leeds. Or when they were up for Lee Gap Fair, that was a three week fair at one time. They've got a square topped wagon and two bow tops.

Tom Kendal

1950's

Annie Kindon

My name is Annie Kindon and I'm seventy-eight years old. I was born in Bawtry, Doncaster.
I was brought up in horses and wagons with me Dad and Mam. I only had one sister called
Mary. She died about three years since, at Doncaster.

...her life in her own words

I think it was much better when I was a child than it is now, really. You hadn't as much money or anything, but things were cheap and stopping was good. You could stop on a roadside for forty-eight hours and they couldn't shift yer, with having horses and wagons - but now they shift you any time. My sister married a collier, so she never travelled, but she wasn't ashamed of it or anything. She'd ride on a horse and cart, she'd come, make herself at home. She wasn't stuck up or anything. She had three children: two boys and a girl. Now she's gone, her husband's gone, and her daughter, there's only the two sons left.

I had a good life and a good husband and a good family. And I travelled all over the place. We enjoyed oursen's. I hadn't a drunken husband or anything like that. He was a good man. And he loved his children and his grandchildren. Their Dad never hit 'em, he only had to talk to 'em, and my oldest, he was twenty-one when he got married, and if he said to him, *"You're not going out of this place tonight"*, he wouldn't go. They wouldn't back-answer their father. They had to be in at a certain time - lads and lasses.

We got married at West Hartlepool, at Christchurch there. We stopped down there for two years and then we come away up here. We've been back since, but I like up here. He belonged the north of England, did my husband. His brothers and sisters were all born down there at West Hartlepool, but we had a good life and there's nowt I could put to it any more, you know.

We never had a lot of money - we never craved for a lot of money. We had four meals a day and where we went the children went with us. If we went to the pictures, we took 'em all with us. They was never left on their own.

I've had good in-laws, good mother-in-law, good father-in-law, sister-in-laws; we were all for one another, and never had a wrong word with 'em. I've got good daughter-in-laws and I like my daughter-in-laws, treated like I like my daughters treated; and my sons-in-law. They'd do anything for me.

We used to have horses. I could drive them, me husband could drive them, he used to drive the wagon sometimes and I'd drive the cart. If he wanted to go for a talk, he'd leave me driving and talk to t'others in front. We used to pull up and have a cup of tea and then finish us journey where we going to after. It was a good life. Travellers were Travellers then, and if you hadn't anything you helped one another. I was married sixty years and I never knowed my husband in any trouble in his life.

And he was well-liked. Even from London, when he took bad, we went down to spend a week with my son, he was down London, and he was badly then like, but Doctor said *"Let him do what he wants"*. So we went and had a week down London, and on the night my son was going out and he said to his Dad *"Are you coming with us for a drink?"* He said *"No"*. I said *"Go on with him"*, but I said *"Don't get him any spirits, don't have any spirits"*, and he didn't and that woman from that Public sent a lovely wreath when he died, you know, and that's first time she'd ever seen him. A big funeral, he had. It's just one of them things. We always said if we ever parted, fall out and parted, we'd never come back, not even for death. And the only time we were parted was when he was in the army.

This is my husband Kazy with his Mam Mary Ann and two sisters Pricilla and Elizabeth Ann in 1919.

This is me havin' me picture taken in Scarborough when I was only fifteen back in 1933.

We had us rows like anybody else; they always say *"True love never runs smooth"*. The only thing me husband and me fell out over was a cigarette - he loved a cigarette. If he hadn't a cigarette and he'd a one hundred pound note, he'd change it for a packet of cigarettes, and he'd ask the King, if he stood there, for a cigarette.

He went off 'em before he died. I used to say to him, because he smoked one sort and I smoked another, and he used to take mine when he had none and that used to cause a row. And I used to say to him *"If you die before me, I'll put you a packet of cigarettes in"*, and I did do that. I didn't put matches in, but I put a packet of cigarettes, ten cigarettes, in the coffin with him. I stuck to me promise.

We were in Barnsley all through t'war, on Queen's Ground. That's where me husband went in t'army, from there. But me Dad belonged Barnsley.

You could get in a farmer's field for a couple of nights. We stopped round Wetherby on the waterside, all round there.

We've been shifted at twelve o'clock at night by the police. We got shifted going to Yarm and we pulled on t'common in Thirsk and they come and shifted us. He had to pull two mile further up the road, at twelve o'clock at night.

OUR FAMILY IN THE EARLY DAYS

This is my husband Kazy with our first son, Arthur, riding on Toby the horse.

IN THE NORTH EAST

This is me and Kazy with our first two children, Arthur and Madge.

These pictures were taken in 1937 when we were stoppin' in the Compound Yard, in West Hartlepool.

It was half-a-crown a week and there was a big wash house.

Ten wagons were allowed in at a time, and some of the Smiths and Pattisons were there with us.

WHEN THE KIDS WERE LITTLE

This is Madge and Arthur when they were little. They are sat on our Bill Wright's wagon that we lived in and we were stopping in the Compound Yard in West Hartlepool in 1938.

Annie Kindon

FOR KING AND COUNTRY 1939

This is Kazy in his uniform, taken at Idle Barracks in Bradford. He has just been called up for the army and we were stopping on the Queen's Ground at Barnsley.

YARM FAIR 1942

Tom and Dinah just went up with an accomodation and dray that year. Dinah is cooking on a 'Milley' in front of their wagon. Tom finished up buying that Leeds built Bill Wright's wagon, on the side, for £70.

Tom gave that German 'Muller' riding whip to Jimmy Tyers, one of the boys. Later, when he was driving a horse called 'Aire Queen', he laid the whip across her. He was arrested for using it to 'race' at Yarm Fair. He got three months for driving a horse at over thirty miles an hour in the High Street!

Jam Jars For Rides in Holbeck, Leeds 1956

This is me husband Kazy and our children, Madge and Arthur, with the ponies and donkey. The children are lining up with used jam jars for a ride on the pony or donkey. Kazy would sell the jam jars on.

You can see the old railway sheds on Ninevah Bridge. We were stoppin' in Morley's Yard near the King's Arms pub. We used to do the 'Donkey Rides' at all the local Galas and Summer Fairs. The children always used to look forward to it.

In Leeds we just stopped on what they called Brown Lane, bottom of Holbeck, just there. And from there, like, we came onto the site. When we were on the camps and we weren't evicted we'd still shift, we just used to go, we never planned the places. We'd have a shift, we'd maybe shift a few mile away - just a few mile, you know. Shift from one side o' road to t'other many a time.

So long as you'd somewhere for horses to graze, you could tether 'em, it wasn't so bad. We used to go with a horse and cart for us shopping, no buses nor nowt we never used to bother with. So many of us would go on one.

There were no electricity, it used to be oil lamps and then they got to Tilly lamps like with a gas mantle, and then they got to gas. Candles - you used to have candles.

We used to have a lot of brassware, copper kettles and such as that. We used to have cast iron pans to cook outside, on the fire. We used to have what you call a kettle prop, and you could hang your pan on, and cook your stuff like that. I used to bake when we hadn't an oven, you used to get little stoves with ovens in, what they called a doctor's stove. Then we got what you call a Queen Anne's stove and I baked on that. I used to bake underneath and on top of the stove, and then put them on the front to brown on the top.

Annie Kindon

I baked Gypsy cake and currant cake in a frying pan cooked on an open fire outside. The currant cake just had currants, lard, just like you mix ordinary pastry, but we had currants in. You could put egg in if you wanted, made it different, you know, any kind of fruit. You can't do it the same on gas it doesn't cook 'em right. You need a fire. I miss cooking outside. Boil us kettle, fry us breakfast, used to eat outside, when it were nice weather we used to have a table outside. And then we bought a tent and used to eat in the tent. Just sleep in the wagon. A good life it was.

There was many a time I've had ten shillings to keep me from Saturday 'til Monday and had bread and everything out of it - bread, cigarettes, all t'lot. You could get three loaves for a shilling in them days, it were only four old pence a loaf. We used to have a fire outside and a singsong. And some'd play a piano accordion, or fiddle, you know. Made our own enjoyment, and it were much better than what it is today.

Camping days is done now, there's no camping like there used to be. When you go to Appleby, Appleby's not the same, it's more of a market than what it used to be, just a horse fair, you know.

We used to go to Appleby, Topcliffe, Yarm Fair, Bakewell Fair, all them places, you know, in Derbyshire. That used to be our holiday. Cooks and dairy maids that's all the women were. The men used to fetch their pals and have a cup of tea, and anybody coming, they were always made welcome.

FARM WORK

Me and Kazy were up picking the fruit in Wisbech in 1971. We had just come out of the fruit fields. We were going to have our dinner and cook on the Primus in the back of the van.

We used to hawk flowers, artificial flowers, wooden flowers, wax flowers, paper flowers or go out gathering old scrap and that, you know.

I used to sit down at six o'clock and I'd twenty dozen flowers made by ten o'clock. You cut them and then you worked your roses with a knife. But the wooden ones were elderberry. You had a special knife to make them with, and then you dyed 'em, you see.

Do 'em all meself and I used to sell 'em at a shilling a piece, in them days. It's five pence today, isn't it? I'd sell them all over, we used to have a week here and a week there.

I've never made any for years now, I wouldn't be bothered now, I wouldn't have the patience but we got us living that way, we had nothing coming in any way only that.

When the Family Allowance came on, I got five shillings a week. It wasn't much, was it? Just the price of a loaf of bread nearly today.

In right olden days, the woman was the worker and the men used to sit at home and make pegs and flowers, for the women to go out. In the right old days. The men works today. Well, my husband always worked. He worked at TNT in Stockton, and he worked for coal men and different jobs he had. He had some good references for working.

We used to go down the fruit, fruit picking, down Wisbech: strawberries, blackberries and apples, plums, gooseberries. I could go now to where we used to go, but it's no good for one, you know, not when you're picking apples; it wants more than one of yer. Climbing trees and that, I'm too old for that now, I like 'em on a plate now!

The children helped with the picking. You start when you want, you could go in at four in the morning if you wanted, the farmers would be there about eight o'clock. You got paid for what you picked. You could earn some good money down t'fruit. It still goes on. Lots still goes down, and that, now. But it's no good for me just on me own. It'd be alright in t'strawberries, but when you come to t'apples, you want more than one. You want someone who can get to t'top of t'trees, climb up t'trees. And I'm not one for heights.

There were strict rules to be followed by mothers when children were born and before they had been 'churched' - Well, they do take 'em out all over now, but we never used to take ours out,'til they'd been christened.'Cos all mine's been born at home, but they never went out the door until they were christened. My Kazy was christened at 3 days old at the Church, used to be at the bottom of Domestic Street, it's a garage now, motor sales. And we never used to touch food until we'd been churched. We could touch it for ourself but not cook for our husband or anything. And our husbands never slept in the bed until we'd been to church.

OUT IN THE FRESH AIR 1977

Me and Kazy were still working in the fields. We were down in Wisbech again, fruit picking in the late seventies.

FAMILY IN LEEDS 1985

This is me son Kazy painting the sides of the lorry. He's with Tracey, Tammy, and Bodean. They weren't long down from London, stopping on the 'Brick Camp' in Holbeck. Everywhere was handy, but it was full of rats. They were on there for two years 'cos there was no room on the council site at Cottingley Springs.

ON THE BRICKCAMP 1985

This shows some of me grandchildren, Thomas, Crimea, Tammy, Heath, Bodean and one of their cousins, Sentbaby, outside Kazy and Tom's trailer in the summertime.

Crimea has got Fred, the chicken. They used to carry him up and down as he had a bad leg and walked lobsided. The children loved him and he'd come in the trailer every morning for the children to feed him.

This is Tom, one of me daughter-in-laws, with some of me grandchildren. There's Tracey, Tammy, Thomas, Bodean, Crimea and Joe.

Story Five

ANNIE AND NELLIE

This is me and Nellie Lowther at a wedding. We were good friends for many years.

The baby girls have their ears done, have 'em done when they're first born, you know. They get 'em done at jewellers now, but they used to do 'em with a cork and a darning needle. But it's much better now because they shoot 'em in with a gun; they don't bleed as much.

My Dad was a good scholar, but I could never pick it up, could never pick reading up. My Dad learnt me Mam to read and write, but no, I can pick anything else up, but I cannot pick reading up. Not 'cos I haven't tried, 'cos I have, but I can't. I can spell odd things but that's all, I can write me name, I can manage that. But all mine's been to school, they can all read and write. Mine all left from Matthew Murray's school. And me grandchildren all go to school now.

I've nothing to grumble at, but I liked travelling up and down, I don't like being stuck on the site. I like to be away. And I think if I still had horses and wagon, I think I'd still be away - some'at I could handle meself, you know; because I was fetched up with horses and I like horses.

Lee Fair, or Lee Gap Fair, at West Ardsley, which has been in the Leeds Metropolitan District since 1974, is the oldest Chartered Horse Fair in England. It is one of the most important events in the Romany calendar and is the largest Horse Fair in Yorkshire, second only to Appleby in the North of England.

It's current Royal Charter was granted by King Stephen in 1136. An earlier Charter was given by King Henry in about 1125, but the Fair's origins probably go back to shortly after the year 867, when Yorkshire was divided by Danish settlers into local government areas called 'Wapentakes'. The Wapentake of Morley, which stretched from Rothwell to Todmorden, met at Tingley, about a half a mile from today's fields. People would make use of the journey by dealing and trading at the meetings.

Originally there were two three-day Fairs three weeks apart. But, probably since 1448, they have been reduced to two one-day events with a gap of three weeks and three days. Gypsies have been coming to Lee Gap since shortly after their arrival in this country in the early 16th century. Because of the unusual gap between the Fairs, many would arrive a few days before the 'First of Lee' and leave after 'Latter Lee', staying about a month in all. Some even stayed on into October for potato picking. In the days of horse-drawn transport, it was not worth going away only to come straight back again. Although this tradition died out when motor vehicles became more common, a small group of bow topped wagons stayed for the full three weeks and three days as recently as 1993.

LEE GAP FAIR IN THE SIXTIES
I've been going since I was a child, with me father.   *Righteous Price*

LEE GAP FAIR BY TOM LEADLEY

Fifty years or more ago, Gypsy children who stayed between the Fairs went to the nearby Westerton School. Until about thirty years ago Hill Top Infants always had a day off school for Latter Lee. Since 1995, Westerton pupils have come to Latter Lee in organised parties and this helps continue the strong links between the local community and the Fair.

My father's parents were regulars at Lee Fair over eighty years ago and I was taken to my first Fair in 1952. At that time, the Fairs did well, with four small fields on either side of Baghill Road. I well remember the bow top wagons on the Gypsy field and Baghill Green with the smokey camp fires and the blackened stew pots and the bare-foot children running about.

Since 1829, when all common land in West Ardsley was enclosed, the Fair has been held by invitation on private fields, and it is remarkable that as one has been closed, another has always been found. Since 1993 I have led the campaign to save the Fair, and we now have an established site once again. Generally, Lee Fair is now a smaller version of Appleby and its closeness to the M62 and the M1 motorways makes it an easy day trip from most of the North of England. There are always some visitors from further afield and others from Wales and Ireland.

Lee Fair is held twice a year, usually on August 24th and September 17th. Charter Fairs cannot be held on a Sunday, and so if the true dates falls on a Sunday, the Fair is held back until the Monday. Most activity is between nine o-clock in the morning and four in the afternoon. There can be no camping now between the Fairs.

LEE FAIR 1998
Latter Lee - showing the hollow where the horse dealing is done.

Lee Gap Fair 1962

YORKSHIRE LIFE ILLUSTRATED 'LEE GAP FAIR JUST WILL NOT DIE' OCTOBER 1962

"A lively pony for sale" - and it proves almost too lively for its handlers.

For 170 years the family of Mr T. A. Bowdler, from Staffordshire, have traded at Lee Gap.

Today, when he makes a sale, the deal is still sealed by the traditional ritual of striking hands.

Age tests age: Bob Farrar, aged eighty-six, from Doncaster takes an expert look at a horse's teeth before he makes an offer.

Lee Gap Fair 1965

Gypsy horses showing their paces at Lee Fair in 1965.

Jimmy Adams selling Welsh ponies which were brought in a drove from Batley station to Lee Fair in 1965.

Tommy Gaskin's wagon camped at Lee Fair in 1965.

Tommy was a famous builder and painter of wagons, but this one is a Bill Wright's wagon, made at his yard in Spibey Lane, Rothwell Haigh, which is now in Leeds.

Lee Fair in the 1990's

Our J.R. and Lucy with a little black rabbit in 1995.

Carrying on the tradition of dealing at Lee Fair. The Price, Knight and Taylor children in 1998.

Me and Paddy Doran sharing a joke on Lee Fair 1998.
We've been coming to Lee Fair all our lives, for horse dealing and trading.

Lee Gap Recorded

Lee Fair's antiquity is remembered in St. Mary the Virgin's Church at Woodkirk. There, in a leaded window with painted panels, the Fair is recorded for posterity.

'This section of the window depicts the church after the roof collapsed in 1831.'

On a wooden plaque dated 1955 in St. Mary's Church

'Woodkirk means wooden church, originally a cell of Black Canons under Nostel Priory, it was formed in the reign of Henry I (1100-1135).'

'A Fair was held at Woodkirk during the reign of Edward II (1284-1327). It was reckoned the most famous in the country, to which it was said, merchants from France, Spain and even Germany came to sell their merchandise.'

"There are some doubts about the reliability of the actual text used on the plaque. For example, Edward II reigned from 1307-1327, not 1284-1327 as written on the plaque. Also, it is more likely that 'continental merchants' came to Woodkirk Fair in order to buy fleeces, and later, woollen cloth, rather than sell merchandise."

Tom Leadley

Anna Lee

Well I'm married now and my name is Anna Lee. There's eight of us in our family, five girls and three boys, I'm the oldest, I'm twenty-nine and the youngest is only six. I was born in Leeds, in 1970 at St. James' Hospital.

80

Story Six

... telling about her life

I've been in Leeds all my life. The only time we really travelled out of Leeds was when we went to Sheffield and Newcastle, but we wasn't there very long. In Leeds we stayed round Cross Green, that's where we were before we come here. I am now living on Cottingley Springs Caravan Site.

Cross Green had no facilities at all, it was like the roadside camps we stayed on. When we first moved on it was like a rubbish tip and we had to clean it up. We camped by ourselves, just our family, 'cos I wasn't married then. It was all factories round there but all the people knowed us with us being around there for so long, so they were alright with us.

From the age of twelve I had me own trailer. I've had about three or four trailers, me last one was a little tourer. Me brothers and sisters had their own trailers as well, so we had four trailers altogether. One for me Mam and Dad, one for the boys, my trailer and then another one for the two girls. As they get to a certain age we don't like boys and girls sleeping in the same room, we like them to have their own privacy. Everybody likes to have their own way of doing things don't they? They don't want brothers and sisters asking 'em "What're you doing there?" and "What're you doing that for?" It's like in a house, everybody has a bedroom each don't they? That's just the same for us, we have a kitchen and the rest is bedrooms.

We don't have toilets and sinks in trailers either, 'cos we think they're very unclean. We never wash in a sink. If we have a sink in the trailer it's always got a dish inside, 'cos we have separate bowls for everything. We have a dish for washing up in, a dish for washing our hands and face in and a dish for wiping around. We never get 'em mixed up. And also when we are doing our laundry we won't wash our tea towels with all the rest of our clothes, 'cos we think that's very unclean - you imagine putting your tea towels in with smelly socks from your feet. After all you've got to wipe up the things you eat and drink off, so that's why we have separate bowls for everything.

On the roadside camps we used to cook inside 'cos we had cookers in the trailers. We had gas from the gas bottles and a generator for electric. We had to go to a cement factory for the water because there was no taps on where we was and for showers we had to go to the sports centre. We'd either go by truck to get our water or me brother'd tow it in a little bogie, a little cart.

We start doing jobs in the trailer from an early age. I learnt all me cooking and cleaning from me Mam, I used to watch her. The girls' chores is looking after the children. While me Mam was doing the washing I'd be looking after the children and then cleaning up. You had to do your share, all the children would have their own jobs to do. The girls had their own routine. Like one would be set to wash up, one would dry and one'd tidy, like take it in turns, on a rota basis. The boys, they'd just do their own thing, they would help me Dad fix the motors or whatever.

We used to keep a few dogs and chickens on the camps. We had the dogs because when you're stopping in a lonely place by yourself you need something near a gate, because there was a gate next to us. And there used to be a lot of people going in and forth that we didn't know, so the dog was like a guard dog really, with little children being there and everything.

Some of the places that we was on, we just got moved off and all that happened after was the sites were just dumped up and left. Now the place where we was for nine years down Cross Green that's just been dumped up and left. They said it was sold and that's why we had to move but all that's been done is it's just dumped up and left. The people who moved us off was just council people. When we was on there and when we thought we had to move first time, one of the councillors come down and said we could

have a bit of land if we had to move, but it never come off. So this was the only alternative we had, to come on the site. We couldn't understand why we were moved after such a long time.

Altogether we was round the Cross Green area, the same area, for seventeen years. Up and down the one road, we seen all the buildings getting put up. We was down Cross Green on one site for 9 years and me Mam asked for a toilet and a skip and they wouldn't put it on. They kept saying *"We can't do it"* and yet there was a camp at Stourton and they put a toilet and a tap on there and a skip. I don't know why, I don't think they wanted us to be there. There was no houses around, just all factories where we was. We was brought up there, we was used to the place. We went to court over the eviction, we were fighting in court for three year for it but they said it was sold. But it's still there, you can go down there today and it's just all dumped up. They've done nowt with it.

People don't get long on the roadside sites now. Not very long, I'd say about a week then they'd get put off but I don't really know, 'cos I really haven't mixed about. Since I've been married I haven't really been from camp to camp. When I was single I used to go and visit my friends a lot but they used to get moved quite frequently. They'd have a week, say now, down Cross Green on the back of fields where we was. Then they'd be moved off, they'd be constantly on the move, so they wouldn't have time to put their children to school or clean rubbish up. When the police comes and say *"We want you off now"*, they just have to go, they wouldn't have time to tidy nothing. So that's why a lot of the time rubbish gets left 'cos they don't have time to clean it up.

CAMPING ON THE ROADSIDE IN CROSS GREEN 1984
Me and me brother Roy with me sisters Sentabel, Nora and Coralina outside our trailer with Aunt Nora and cousins William and Serianne.

WORKING FOR TRAVELLERS EDUCATION SERVICE
Giving a talk at Leeds University. Sentabel, me and Sakie.

I've never been to school. There's a team called 'Travellers' Education' they were the ones that started coming around and learning me how to read and write. Well I think a good education helps you a lot, 'cos if you can't read there's not a lot of jobs you can get. When my girl gets to the age of schooling we're going to put her in school and hopefully if she wants to get a job, then if she's got education she can get a job. You've got to be able to read and write, that's why I think education is very good.

Like them training schemes they're very good again. I was on one of them, training for clerical work and I did get a job at the end of that. I went to work at Travellers' Education and the course helped me a lot, to do the things in the office. I worked with Travellers' Education for three years but before I went there I worked in a popcorn factory down in Cross Green. I was the first of my brothers and sisters to go to work. None of them were working then because they was all young when I started working.

It wasn't very easy for me when I was looking for a job. The first job I ever went for, it was only for £50 a week, packing light bulbs. I goes to this factory down in Cross Green and I was the only person that turned up 'cos I knew the girl from the estate who worked there, so I goes for the job. He told me I had the job and to ring back Friday for them to let me know what they was doing. So they said *"Can I have your address?"* I knew it was me address: *"Caravan Site, Cross Green"* why I never got the job. So there was prejudice there, that's why I never got it, so that's when I went to the college.

I have two sisters that are working, one's working in a school and another one's working in a factory. Me sister went on a training course, then she started going into schools. A job come round for someone to go to a school and she went for the interviews and she got a place, so she took that. Me other sister, some of the other girls on the site here got jobs at the factory so she went to the agency and she got one.

When I was smaller I came across a lot of prejudice but there's not so much today. You know like calling names and that, *"Smelly Gypsy"* and getting stones thrown at you. You cope with it by... you just tell them off basically, that's the only way you can cope with it. You just tell 'em that you're just as good as them and the only difference is that you live in a caravan, 'cos there's no other difference at all, is there? That's what you do basically. I think if people actually got to know Travellers instead of just writing stuff and reading what they say in the papers then they'd have a different story. There might be people that don't even know Travellers and they read whatever they say in the papers about 'em and then they just go by that. So, when they see Travellers they'll start calling names and things because they don't know who they are, 'cos they don't know them as a person they just know them from what they read. But I think it's getting easier, Travelling children's going to school, learning to read and write. When I was small there wasn't hardly no Travelling girls working. But now they're giving them chances, they're recognising that they're good workers when they do get jobs and that they're getting a chance to prove themselves, like I did. So yes, it is getting better.

In the olden days, long before my time, Travellers used to make pegs and flowers and go round hawking, some still goes out hawking today. The men made the pegs and the women went and sold the flowers and some used to go round the houses reading the palms or the crystal. The men would do rags or sell horses - that was their main trade in the old days, selling horses and carts and swapping motors and doing trailers. Horses were important in them days, now its trees, tarmacking and whatever you can get really. To some, horses are still important, it's what's been passed down to them, what they're still carrying on. I've got an uncle who's got a lot of horses.

Appleby is a big fair, once a year, it falls on the first week in June and Travellers from all over the country come. It's on for a week but some pull on two weeks before time. I went to Appleby once or twice when I was a child and I've been when I was married. We just went to see the families and do a bit of shopping up there, that's where you get all your fancy cushions and that. Appleby came early this year and there was a lot more trailers on. There was hardly space to put your motor beside your trailer. It's mainly families coming to meet up with each other from different parts of the country.

They also go to sell horses, it's mostly a man's fair 'cos a lot of horse dealing and stuff goes on. Thousands of horses got sold at Appleby this year. One man brought thirty-odd horses there and sold the lot. Horse dealing is a very skilful business. People'll always try to be wise and bid a lot lower than what the

APPLEBY FAIR 1997

horse is worth but they're not going to sell them for a lot less than what they want for them, 'cos they're thoroughbreds see. They trot the horses up and down to test the best horse, to see how they work, to see the value of the horse. That's to get men interested in buying them. To see what the horses looks like and what they actually can do, 'cos if they're no good at keeping their feet at a certain pace they're no good for trotting. That's when you get a top quality horse, when it's a good trotter and its legs is going the same as the other ones, at the right pace.

This year the lake at Appleby where they wash the horses was completely full and a little boy actually fell off and broke his leg. They're trying to stop the young Travellers riding the horses down the road and washing them in the river but the council said they couldn't because it was tradition - since the fair's been going they've been washing the horses in the stream, so they couldn't stop it. And they've tried to do away with Appleby Fair but they can't 'cos it was royalty that opened that fair up in the first place.

They have a big market at Appleby as well and the women go to buy themselves clothes and treat the children to some new shoes and things. You get really pretty things there.

There's a few fairs but we don't go to many, we've been to Appleby and Stowe on the Wold. There's fairs at Epsom, Lee Gap and Newcastle.

The fairs are important 'cos if you haven't seen your family from one side of the country, from one year to the next, they gives you time to catch up on old times and on new families starting up. You see all your relations. It surprises you when you see all your relations there 'cos there's some of them you don't even know, coming from all different countries, so it's really nice. At Appleby they mainly talk about all the happy stuff, the old times there, you know, the old stories.

JOHNNY EAGLE 'STRONGMAN'
Breaking chains at Appleby Fair.

They all meet up in the pub to sing. The women'll go to one pub and the men'll go to another. And the men'll be singing in that pub and the women'll be singing in that pub and meet all up on the way home and have a good old sing song coming on the way home. Sometimes they sing Traveller songs, very old ones, like their grannies and granddads used to sing. They're passed down so it's really nice, like old memories coming back.

There is a man at Appleby that breaks chains, he gets this big horse chain with very very big links and he wraps it round himself. He actually breaks the chain off the lock and he gets out of it. It's good to see is that. He's getting past it now though. I couldn't believe it when I seen the size of the chain. He swallows razor blades and all that sort of thing.

Travellers follow routes round the country. After Appleby they'll pull somewhere else and then go to another thing and it's getting like that with the Christian tents. It's the same with the Christians. We went to the Christian Convention in London and it was lovely.

It's just like a load of Gypsy people come to worship God in a tent. We have Gypsy pastors, that's actually been to college and passed all the exams. Proper pastors, they're fully trained. So it's just like a church really but they have a big tent. All the Travellers come from all over and gather in one place.

Again it's just like Appleby Fair getting to know each other, but there you go to worship God not to horse deal. There's many more people, like old relations getting together on there. Some of 'em have got too old to travel to the horse fair so they meets up at the Christian Convention.

It is really good to know that we have got Travelling people doing the same as everybody else but it really doesn't make a difference if you go to them or the other church down the town. The Gypsy pastors are helping other Travellers in Romania. They gather little parcels up, like food parcels and all sorts and take them over there. The congregation made parcels up, everybody donated a parcel, to give their bit to take over to Romania. There's lots of Gypsies over there, lots of other tribes.

The church we go to isn't a Travelling church it's just a normal church. Travellers and housed people, there's a mixture of each.

Travellers' weddings are usually very big. The first child's christening and your wedding. I had eight bridesmaids at my wedding. Me dad asked me if I wanted to have a church wedding but I didn't want a church wedding. I had it in a register office but I still had the trimmings and everything - eight bridesmaids, best woman, best man, pageboys, it was very nice.

We had the 'do', the reception, afterwards in a pub. All my family and all my husband's family came and there were a lot of outsiders there too.

Christenings are usually big do's. Me and me husband's Christian so we got our daughter dedicated in a Christian church. Importance of faith depends on who they are. They can follow it the way they want to, take it up as well as they want to, but I think God's got an important place in your life and he helps you in a lot of ways. So if you're going to believe in anybody you should believe in God, that's what I say.

GYPSY AND TRAVELLER CHRISTIAN CONVENTION

Everyone comes from all over for a week. They have all the meetings in the big tent and they have Gypsy and Traveller preachers. There is no trouble. They sing Christian songs and it is lovely.

Today, Travellers dress the same as anybody else. It used to be old pinnies and plaid skirts and scarves in their hair but not today, they just want to be counted the same as everybody else. It's true they do like bright colours and fancy things. They do like jewellery, it gets passed down from family to family. The oldest girl'll get something off yer Mam and then you give it to your oldest girl, so things gets passed down. I've got pearl beads that me Dad give me when I was small, so I'll give 'em to my girl when she gets older. That's important 'cos then you've showed you got something old to give 'em that's worth something in their time to come.

The collecting of Crown Derby goes back to olden times. The husband'd buy it for the wife and then she'd put it up. We've got some, the biggest half of Travellers today've got Crown Derby in all shapes and forms. I think they like it for it's bright colours and the way it's decorated, they are beautiful colours. Plus when you've got cabinets like this in your trailer it's something to make 'em stand out more, instead of bare sideboards, just fill them up with fancy things and it makes your home look a lot more homelier.

The Romanes language is still very important, it's still used by Travellers in the talking, in most of the speech they use it. So far as I believe it originated from India and it's a very old language called Sanskrit. There's all different tribes and each one speaks it differently, there's Zincali, Benechtay and there's the Kalderash and Manouche. They speak all different tongues but certain things they would be able to understand. The Scotch is called Cant and Irish is Gammon so they're different again. Travellers still use it to talk to one another. Like our little girl now she's five month old, she'll be learning it so she can pass it down to her children. Each child that's born, they learn the Romany language so they pass it on to their children. If people's there that we don't know, we'll use English as well with it, but when we're by ourselves we can speak it then.

The sites they're making now's too big, too crowded and they're miles out from anywhere. Now if a poor person never had a motor on this site, look how far they'd have to go to the shops, down to Hunslet or up to Morley, now that's a long walking distance. But unless you're on the site now you've got nowhere to go because that new law's been passed and they can evict you and take your home off you if you don't move when they tell you to. I haven't seen any sites that are better than this one, they've all been overcrowded, the ones I've seen, too many people on them. They're all crowded but this is alright, but it's still too big. They should make family sites or ten plots, but they won't do that.

If I could make me own site, I'd make a family site, I'd make ten plots and I'd make it somewhere the children could play 'cos there's no play area or nothing on here. I'd also make it like a double plot so they had a bit more space for the motor and vehicles. I wouldn't put it out in the wilderness, I'd make it somewhere where you could be seen. I'd put an amenity shed on it with a toilet, a bathroom, tap outside and a kitchen area, just like the ones on here.

It would be better if they asked Travellers about how to build the sites. It would be much better. If they sat down with the Travellers they wouldn't spend as much money as what they do on the sites. 'Cos they wouldn't ask for the world, all they'd ask for would be a shed to be built with amenities in it, a plot, a fence up and lights around. On here, look all the lights is not working. They'd want a biggish plot 'cos when you've got a big family you have more caravans and they don't realise that. They make all the plots all narrow to fit one trailer on and then they expect people to fit their family on. 'Cos when you got a family you need that bit of extra room.

Travelling people still want to travel 'cos it's like a part of their life going back. But now if they're not on a site that's it, they're done.

Me mother-in-law's actually bought her own piece of land, but it hasn't been passed and she might have to move. They've made like a proper site in Lofthouse, they've made it to their own liking and everything. But they're not getting nothing else done with it 'cos they've got to wait to see what happens. If the council would let them people stay there, they would build it up themselves. They've put a toilet amenity on it, they've stoned it all out, they've put outside taps on it, they've put electric on it, so they're paying electric and everything but they still might all get put off and lose all their money. That's it, they've nowhere to go and that's a bit of land going to waste.

IN OUR TRAILER 1993

Charles and Sheralee with their cousin John. The picture was taken for the Labour Party as part of their campaign for Traveller's Rights to try and make stopping easier.

THE FUTURE - OUR ANNA WHEN SHE WAS ONE 1997

We want our daughter to be classed as everybody else, not to be pointed out. We want her to be classed as a human being and to be like everybody else. We don't want her to be treated any different.

Like probably in the future there won't be no sites left, we'll probably end up in houses. I'm sad about that 'cos the way things is working out they're doing away with all the Travelling life, the way we were brought up, to be travelling around. They're doing away with a part of our life. Like even though me meself I never travelled much until I got married, I still like to think I could go to a camp and pull on it whenever we got moved from another one. But now you can't, you can't do that now. So that's all gone, all the happiness of seeing the green pastures where you were pulled. Instead now it's just all dumped up and lots of rubbish tipped everywhere. It's great to be able to just go off when you want. But like I said it's coming to an end, slowly but surely.

I don't really know how I'd feel about going into a house 'cos I never been in a house so I couldn't really say. You see I've always been in a trailer. It's like saying to a person who lives in a house *"Would you like to move out of your house and you have my caravan?"* I don't think they'd like it, would they?

Well that's what they wanted, they offered me Mam houses you know when we had to shift off that other ground. One in Chapeltown and one in Halton Moor, nothing with gardens. *"We can give you a house"* - they were trying to say we was homeless. How could we be homeless when we live in a trailer? We explained it to 'em but they still class you as homeless 'cos you live in a trailer.

And then I said to them *"Wouldn't you think yous'd give 'em to yer own people when there's people out there living in cardboard boxes in Leeds town centre"*. I said *"Why don't you give the houses to the people that really need 'em?"* I said *"We've got a home"*. I said *"Them poor people haven't"*, but no further forward. So that was it.

The Boswell Family

'This is a kushti varda.'

(Romanes)

Me father, Greensie Boswell, made this living wagon and painted it. He brought the wagon and horses from Ireland when he came over in the 1950's.

His father before him was a builder and joiner of wagons. They did jobs for Travelling people: rejoining wagons and carts and painting them.

They had the designs for painting from years ago.

He loved doing the fruitwork, carving out the grapes.

He painted the wagon and lined it out and scrawled it.

This is the family in the same wagon at Yarm Fair in 1957.

...just thinkin' back

MAY BOSWELL'S RECOLLECTIONS

BALLINA COUNTY MAYO 1952
There's me, May, and me two sisters, our Margaret and our Lucy.
My Mam had just died.

DUBLIN BRICKWORKS CAMP 1953
There's me sister, Susie, with Rene Lock, they used to travel up and down with us in the old wagons. There's also me sister, Lucy, when she was a child, with me brother, Pa and Reggie Clarke. Me father was making that wagon at the time. The camp was by the chocolate facory and there was a big football field up the back.

BIRMINGHAM 1954
Taken when we'd first come over. We used to go out hawking and for a laugh we'd go into the photo shop. Sometimes they'd do us some of the photographs for nothing. I was only fourteen.

EVESHAM 1956
Holly, Suzie and me and the two horses. We were picking fruit. We'd just come over from Ireland.

SOUTH YORKSHIRE, 1958
That's me sister-in-law Bina Carty, she's married to me brother, Holly and there's Dunion Young, Mary's husband and me father, Greensie sat by the fire with me brothers, Alfie and Pa and Geordie White. It was taken on Dinnington Commons where Dolly me daughter was born in 1958. Everyone stopped on there for years.

Bobby Lee

My full name's Bobby Lee. I was born in a little village near Sunderland called Easington Lane. I was born 24th December 1928 in a wagon in a lane. We travelled about ever since, until I got married.

...telling of his life and times

Yes, my Dad were a full Lee, you see, a full Gypsy - a full Lee. His mother were a Lee and his father were a Lee. Jonina was my grandad, and Nancy were me grandmother. Ada North's grandfather and my grandmother were brother and sister.

Such as us, we can only go back a couple of generations. I go back to my grandmother - but in my Dad's family, they were a big family and they were all Travelling people and they settled down. There were about eight in their family, but there were only two girls in it - two women. All the rest were lads. Same as me Mam's family. My Mam was married when she was seventeen - she was married young - and she had ten children, five lads and five lasses.

●

I speak Romanes. It's not Romany, it's Romnness. We're Romanichals - we're not Romanies. I'm a Romanichal. A Gypsy in your saying should be a Romanichal, we're Gypsies, Romanichals. I'd accept that word. I'm a Gypsy, yes. The old end. If anybody came to me and said *"What nationality?"* I'd say *"I'm a Gypsy"*. You see, when you talk to an old Romanichal, such as me and Ada and them, what's left, we're the old 'uns now. We're proud of being Gypsies.

We travelled the roads all us life, like, and you've got to leave the places clean because you know you're going to come back to stop again. And the way they get a bad name about thieving and one thing and another, they weren't thieves, weren't Gypsies. No.

●

We always had trailers, you know. You know what a trailer is - a living trailer. And me Dad could drive a motor, like. We were in motoring trailers from very young, when I were very young, and the only time we went back into horse and wagons were during the war, when you couldn't get petrol - horse and wagons we went into, until the war finished, and then we were back into trailers again. Always had a good trailer and that. That was one good thing about us - we always had a good feather bed to lay on.

●

If your Mam and Dad told you to do something, in them days, it had to be done. You never looked back or answered back. No *"I'll do it in a minute"* or *"I'll do it after"*. You had to get up there and then and do it there and then. You were fetched up that way. And you were fetched up to respect other people, and other people's things. If anybody asked you *"Would you fetch us a can of water, Bobby?"*, you'd get hold of a can and, if it were 2 mile, you'd go for a can of water and fetch it back, and you wouldn't dare take a penny off 'em. That was just the way you were fetched up, to do for other people, and to respect old people. No back words - no cheek back to 'em.

●

When we were little, we were travelling a lot round Middlesbrough and Stockton, with horse and wagons, and we went to school. That was a strict rule of me mother. If we stopped in a place we went to school. Even when we went to Fairs - such as Topley Fair - we went to school there. If we were there a week, we had a week in school. Never made any good scholars of us, like, but that's what we did. We went there and we travelled from Fair to Fair, and me Dad were a horse dealer - made a quid off a horse here and there, like. And me Mam used to go out with flowers, and a basket with a bit o' lace, or a comb and one thing and another in it, from door to door. We made flowers when we got a bit older.

●

The first Fair we travelled to was Darlington on Easter Monday, and from Darlington we followed the Fairs round, and there was Appleby, we used to go to Appleby, then we'd come back down to Boroughbridge Fair. That was the week after, the Tuesday after Appleby, Boroughbridge. And when we were all small we run about. It was a different time o'day as it is today, like. As long as you had a belly full and a good shelter over your head and good bed you were happy. Whereas today they're not happy with owt, are they?

Then we'd leave there and wait for the next Fair and pull in a lane, and I used to take one end of the lane and me brothers would take the other end, and we'd tend the horses. We were up there all day, and just stop them from getting out one end and stop them from coming out the other end, like. That was more or less our life until we got older - looking after horses. Aye, I liked the horses. I suppose when you're fetched up with a thing, like.

This is what sent you to sleep on a night time, were the rain on the open top, like, the sheet. Yes, it used to send you to sleep. Up early the next morning to recover the horses out of the field you used to put them in! Well, you used to sit in the lanes 'til dark watching them, and then when it got dark you used to put 'em in a farmer's field and get them next morning before the farmer got up, like, and the same thing again. And you got stopping in lanes for ages without bother, because them days the people - the old women themselves - were a lot cleaner and tidier than they are today, because when you left a place you left it as you found it. You couldn't find a matchstalk when we used to move, and where the fire had been, cut another sod out and put it on top and cover the fireplace up and just leave it as you found it. And you could always go back - you were always welcome back, like, you know.

Seacroft Common, up here, we used to pull on there regular - a fortnight - and then they used to come and say, *"It's about time you had a move"* and we used to move, and clean up, and always could go back a month or so after, and they never bothered yer. But I think the Law were a lot easier on you in them days than they are today, because they hound you today, don't they, whereas they used to come up on their bicycle in them days. And they used to say, *"Time you were moving. How long are you going to stop?"* or something like that, and if you said, *'Two or three days,'* you were alright, and they expected you to move on, so everything were alright.

Then in between times, me Mam used to go out with a few flowers, and a basket, like, and one thing and another, and that's how we used to live. There were no 'help-outs' like there is today, you had to earn all you got. And we run around with us trouser's arse hanging out and stocking heels out, but we got over it, we'd a good life. They say the 'Good old days'; it weren't so good, but it were easy like, we got through it.

We travelled with everybody. We travelled with old Joe Varey and his family, there was old Tom Lister, we travelled with them, old John Brough from Easington. We travelled with all the Gypsies like, all of 'em, and they all got on together - there were no falling out.

They all used to help one another in them days. Whereas today they don't bother, but in them days they all used to help one another, and I remember when I were a little young'un, at Topley Fair. A horse got in the beck at Topley, in the river, and drowned, and I've seen me Dad go round collecting from wagon to wagon, so that man would have something to start with, to get off, but they don't do it today. To buy another cheap old horse to pull him about, like. But they don't seem to do it these days.

My Dad, Bobby Lee, bickinin' or kinin' a grai in the kitchima yard.

(Romanes)

BOROUGHBRIDGE FAIR IN THE 1940'S

You got on, and there were good times, we'd sit down lanes and that, but still, there was no telly anyway, was there, in them days, not sixty year ago there wasn't, anyway. We'd be at Darlington, up a lane called Catkill Lane. We used to stop up there for a week in and week out, and we'd walk that five mile from Catkill Lane to Darlington to go to the pictures, and walk back. That was a part of the entertainment, more or less.

My Dad was called Bobby Lee. He used to do a bit of dealing, he was a bit of a comedian like. They called him Popeye because he had a bit of a seizure, years ago, and it closed his eye, like, and he kept his hand over his eye most of the time, more or less, and that's what they called him Popeye for. And it carried on till he died, yes. Everybody used to know him by it. I got Muskra. I don't know meself how I got it, 'cos I had it from being very small. Somebody give me it in fun and it stuck and that were it. I carried it for years, till me Dad died more or less. When he died I got Bobby.

Oh, we got used to going to school at different places, you see. It didn't seem to bother you. You sat there and you listened to what they said and you tried your best to cope with it. And later on in life, when we got a little bit older, there was a school teacher, you know, used to come round with a bus. They called her Aunty Brown. She was from Northallerton. And she used to come round teaching us - teaching all the Travelling people. I'd be seven or eight year old. About sixty year ago.

We always used to come back to Leeds in winter, and we used to go into Potters Field, over at Hunslet there. We used to pull in Potters Field and there were Varley & Pearson - two partners - and they were coach painters. And through the winter she used to put the trailer into Varley & Pearson's and have it all painted and that, and we used to get a house in Potters Field and stop there till Easter. And then we used to move on again and then come back again. I went to Ingram Road School, that's over Carr Lane, and I went to Princess Field School - it's still up is the school but it's Offices and that now. I went to Sweet Street School, that were at the bottom of Princess Field - it's a Gas Board place now - and St. Matthew's, that was on Holbeck Moor, facing the church, it used to face the church. I went to a few schools in Leeds, different winter times. We wouldn't have a regular attendance there, like, or be a regular pupil can I say. Winter time, if we got near a school, we went to a school. Or through the summer, if we stopped in a place and we knew we were going to stop a fortnight or three weeks, we'd be at school. I never learnt to read and write. I can read a little bit now, with reading comics when I left school. Yes, and to write. I write as I talk. No full stops, commas, or owt like that. I just write as I talk. Well, she could fathom out what I were talking about, writing about, would Pat.

This is me when I was nineteen.

Well, I left home when I were thirteen year old. I'd had enough like. So I left home when I was thirteen. I came back up to Leeds - we were in Hartlepool at the time - and I came back up to Leeds. Me Dad and Mam were parted for years, like, but he always travelled with us. And he were in Leeds this time and me Mam were at Hartlepool, and I got fed up, we had words, so I come back to Leeds to me Dad. And I stopped in Leeds and run about Leeds with me Dad for a while, and he went back up north and I come back down here. And I went in the army from down here. I done two year in the army, come home, got courting and I married Pat.

I went in the army 'cos it was conscription at the time. You had to do your eighteen months. But I was greedy and I got to stop demob for six months. I'd two year to do. That would be 40's. I was nineteen at the time. I should have gone in at seventeen but I was nineteen. And I come out - I think it were 1947. In the army it was terrible, 'cos you know, not being used to being told what to do and what not to do, you can't do this and you can't do that. When you can't read you're lost in the army, 'cos people, when they've nowt to do they sit and read a book. I couldn't. It were a hard time for me. I was glad to be out. I was stationed at a place called Winbourne, near Poole in Dorset. I was in the Catering Corps there.

I came back to Leeds. Got on with Pat and settled down. Well I don't know, I think I'd had enough of it. I got a job. It was a big change, but when I got married, you see, I took responsibilities on, and if you remember, in 1950 and '51, it were like a depression on. You couldn't get work. I even went down the pit for six months to keep my family. Then I come up and a got a job at West Riding Paper Service, and I were there for about twenty years or so. I finished there and started working for Hargreaves.

I've just come out of the army and I'm stopping in Leeds with me cousin, Eddie James.

I was always a wagon driver. I was working for Hargreaves on tipping wagons, and William Peppers - I worked for them for about eighteen months - and I started working, doing a bit of haulage from the Wholesale Market down to the Retail, and I had that job for fifteen or sixteen years. That's been my life until I had heart attacks and then I finished.

I got on alright with non-Travellers. I mean to say, you get on alright with people if they're alright with you. It's just a matter of life, isn't it? I married a non-Traveller anyway. It didn't bother me, it didn't bother any of us.

Our Bobby now says to me *"Why don't you go and mix with your own?"*, but it doesn't bother me, you see, I'm content as I am. When you've spent the biggest part of your life at it, you've had enough of it, haven't you. It's nice to come home and sit in comfort. When I go out now and get wet through, I come home, change me clothes and I'm dry. When you're in them small wagons you couldn't. You were there changing your clothes, but you were still out in the rain more than likely.

This is me and Pat at Harry Craddock's wedding in 1949.

It's a good life, what we used to call a Romany life, it's a good life, if you're fetched up to it. You've got to be fetched up to owt like that, I think.

My grandchildren will remember because, such as Bobby, he's took to it, and Ada's family there. But my family, there's only him who's took to it. But they know what they are. No. I don't think any of my own family will go back on the road now, will they, because there's nothing for them. Once upon a time you could come down here, up the road here, what they call Seacroft Common, and stop there. You could go down Brown Lane, there was a big Common on Brown Lane, years ago, with a few pigstys and one thing and another. You could stop there for a week or so, stop on the Lemming for a week or so - not far from Brown Lane, but there's nowt like that now. You've got to be pulled on a concrete block. You might as well be in a house, comfortable in a house, as be in a trailer on one of them places.

Today you can jump into a car. Appleby you can do in two or three hours. So why do you want to travel all the way up there just for the Fair Day. In them days, when we used to go, it was to earn a living. You were earning a quid off a horse or some'at else you used to sell. Today they just go up to say they've been. *"I've been to Appleby for the day out"*. They're going for the outings not to keep theirselves, to live, you know. All these Fairs, years ago, they were made to earn your living. They weren't made for a day's holiday or going to show your things off and one thing and another. You used to go to earn a shilling, to keep your family. It's a lot different, times have changed.

If I take it into my head I'll go to Appleby for a day, like. You recognise people, even if you haven't met 'em for donkey's years. Everyone knows one another and they won't have met for donkey's years, but they know 'em. Now today, you see more people that you know at funerals than you do anywhere else. They've come to pay their last respects, and you go to pay your last respects, and you meet people, it's the only places today, you meet a lot of people that you've known for years.

There were quite a few characters when I was young. There was old Pat Lee. Now old Pat Lee, he were a character on his own, 'cos he could neither read or write, and he were a man of substance, plenty of money in his pocket, and he could play any tune on a melodeon - a jig or any tune at all, he only had to hear it once and he could pick it up and play it and never had a lesson in his life. Then there were old Ernie - that were old Pat's brother. They were deaf as door nails annorl.

There was music and singing. But not like you see on the telly and the films. They never sang and danced about like that. They used to sing to entertain theirselves. They used to sing to one another and entertain theirselves - in Public Houses and on Fairs. There's still some on Fairs. But not like it was. Some would sing a song and then someone else would sing a song. Just to keep the company going. But on them Fairs, what they got together for was 'cos they were dealing up. They were earning a shilling. And years ago, there wasn't such a thing as a woman going in a Public House, when I were a lad. It's only the younger end what's got into going out with their husbands in Publics.

Years ago, before I were born, do you know Ninevah Bridge, there's a Library on the corner, well facing that Library there's a wall on the Railway banking, that used to be called Craven's Yard, and all the Gypsies used to stop in there when I was a babby. They used to pull in there for winter time.

Pickle Yard in Domestic Street, was a Showman's Yard. Showmen used to stop, and some of the Blackpool Gypsies used to stop there. Well, that's where they originate from, where such as us, we come from Middlesbrough, my Dad comes from Middlesbrough and Stockton and that way on.

Biggest part of 'em spoke the same Romanes as we spoke. But they had a different way of living, a different going on than we have. There were a few of 'em worked for the showmen, like, you know. What you call a 'showman's lackey'. But we always went out and earned us own few shillings.

I had a brother, Billy and two sisters, Nancy and Helen, born on the Brick Fields. That were over Armley, up past the gaol, further up. Opposite Armley Park. It were a brickyard, that had been flattened down, and it were like a big field, and they all used to stop in rows on it. You could stop the winter time on the Brick Fields. There were tents - people had barrows who lived on the Brick Fields - with a barrow and made a tent up, yes. Well, Nancy's four year older than me, I were only a young person. It was finished more or less when I were born. Well, I were born in 1928, so you can see how old I was, if it finished in the 30's.

The people would find somewhere else. They'd take to the roads again and find somewhere else. Same as Barnsley, there used to be a place at Barnsley they all used to stop, and I can't think of the name of it now. They all stopped on there. If you ask anybody who knows Barnsley, they'll tell you. And it were like the Brick Fields, there were loads stopped on there. They used to stop up and down the waterside at Otley. They stopped at Aberford Common, where the North Road used to run the side of. We all stopped on there, and Micklefield Common.

We stopped on all these old Commons, and they could stop a week or so, but they won't let you stop today. Them days you could stop a week or a fortnight. But when we stopped on Brown Lane, we had to go to Ingram Road School, every day. That were her - while we were on there, owt near a school, we were at school.

Travellers who stopped at Castley years ago, it were old Bill Wilson and his family. They stopped down there on that waterside. Everybody had their own little bits of stopping places, like they'd stop a fortnight and then they'd know they'd have to move and they'd go somewhere else.

You see, I remember in Leeds here, when we were on Brown Lane and me Dad used to come down

behind Leeds Market, on what they called the Muck, behind Leeds Market, where the Bus Station is, more or less. That used to be a big Muck, and there were boards all the way round it, and they used to do a bit of dealing on there. Tappers' Market they used to call it. All the Tappers used to pull on, with stuff on their carts, and people used to come, like a Car Boot Sale, and buy the stuff off 'em. And it were all horse and carts them days. Wagons on the road in them days when I'm going back were all on solid tyres. Solid wheels.

And when we were going up to Appleby, I can remember being a lad going up to Appleby, and there were chain-driven wagons, with t'fires in front, steam-driven, car wagons. They were bad roads them days, little narrow roads, up to Appleby. Now they're big broad roads.

It's 1970 and I'm on Appleby Fair with me brother, Georgie, and friend, Arthur Hall.

We're stood in front of me Mam's trailer.

Going up to Appleby or them places, there might be up to a hundred, going on the road, all at once, some stopping in one lane, some stopping on the moorside before you got up to Appleby. Scotch Corner were your first stop, then you'd go on up to Bowes and stop on Bowes Corner or in Bowes Quarry, from there you'd go up to Smallways, that were big broad road corners where they cut through for the road, and then you'd get to Keswick Beck bottom, that was just the other side of Brough, and then you were into Appleby.

We used to come from Appleby to a dance at Brough, in the town centre. As you're coming out you used to go up a bit of a bend up a hill, and then you'd come to the moor on the top. You went through Brough to Brough Hill to where they held the Fair, near Warcup. Today it's all them army tanks and that on the right-hand side, as you go. And there used to be a little broad corner with a little beck running through it. They used to call it Keswick Beck Bottom. We used to stop there for a day or two, before we went up, fatten the horses up, like, you know.

It was a good life, there was a lot of fun in it when you were younger; running about, a lot of fun in it. But you had to make your own enjoyment and fun in them days. Nowerdays they go looking for everything.

A living wagon was a vardo. Accommodation was just like four bows over a flat cart and a sheet over it. A rully is a four-wheeled vehicle, and a flat cart's a two-wheeled. You could put accommodation on a rully or a flat cart. If you had it on a flat cart, they always stuck the shafts through hedge, to keep it level, to keep it straight so that your bed was straight.

There was three or four different things. There was a bow-topped wagon, there was an open wagon, there was a wagon called a sleeper. It was like an open lot, but it had the front in, it hadn't the sheets in. They call that a sleeper. I don't know why, but that's how they come. That's a Readin' wagon up there - a square-sided wagon.

It's A Kushti Varda What He's Done

(Romanes)

That's my Uncle Jimmy, my cousin Kizzy and my Aunt Clara, who was my dad's sister.
This could be an Open Lot he's just finished. He used to build them, paint them and line them.

It's A Kushti Varda What He's Done

We always had open lots, and years ago a Bill Wright's wagon, when they were cheap enough. They're too expensive now, like.

Bill Wright's was here in Leeds. There were two brothers. Just outside Rothwell, there. They were great wagon-builders you see. Biggest part of the Travelling people, the Romanies, used to go and order wagons built off them. It might take 'em twelve months to build one, but they were the best builders. He did square sided wagons annorl, did Bill Wright. Yes, they were good builders.

Jimmy, me Uncle Jimmy, he were one of the biggest painters - Jimmy Berry. He painted that one in York Museum, you know. He's dead now, God rest his soul, but he was one of the top painters in my time, when I were a lad. People would fetch their things and leave them with him, and he'd tell them when it would be done. I've no idea how he learned to paint. They didn't get no training, or owt like that, and he were a marvellous painter. He could paint a scroll on the side of an open top or a wagon, and it were just like a transfer, and it were a painting. And a horse - he could paint a horse, and it were real, just like it were stood there, and if it were big enough it were a real horse, it were that natural.

They had him on that programme, "What's my Line?". But they found out who he was. They got him. He married my Dad's sister, my Aunt Clara.

Well, the people wanted the best, same as Bill Wright's wagons were the best, and one time Eccles trailers were the best, and they all had them. Well when that come to be Royal Crown Derby, that was what the royalty went and bought. That's how it came to be Royal - they got the Crown on it and the lot - so people started buying that then. What it is, it's as good as having money, 'cos you can take it anywhere and sell it. It's an investment.

Well, you see, I got mine from my Mother when I got married, and I suppose when she went out hawking and that, and she come across a budiker with it in, she'd go in and she'd put so much on it, and every time she went past the shop she'd put so much on it until she'd paid for it.

Travellers all have big funerals. It's a bit of respect they show for one another, you see. It's just a respect. The gorgis don't do it, do they? There's five or six will go, and they don't sit up all night, three or four nights before they bury 'em. I remember sitting around a fire while a coffin were in a tent or in the wagon when I was young.

They sit up just to be with 'em and show their respect for the last few days, same as when Jesus died, it's a three days' mourning. It wasn't a mourning - they said he rose again on the third day, didn't he. Well this is what they sit for. Respect, yes.

This is me and Pat enjoyin' ourselves in 1987. We were on holiday in Benidorm with Ada, Madgie K, Barry and Gloria.

The Price Family

This is me Dad, Righteous, with young Dawn, me sister, stopping in Cosby, Leicestershire, back in 1969.

Me Mam, Tilly, was telling fortunes on there, on Epsom Downs, for the races. We had an old Eccles trailer. We'd given up the wagon and horses, they were finished then. There's me, Vi and Kevin in 1964.

I'm with me oldest boy, Shugs here. He's on the hobby horse at Skegness. We were all workin' up there in 1971.

...just remembering

Atchin' on a kushti tan, well aye, in this bora gav.

(Romanes)

This is me and me wife Tilly. She's got Bullerman in her arms, We're with Righteous, Linda, Elvis and Dawn. We were camping on a ground in Hunslet, Leeds in 1984.

This is me and me grandchildren, Shugs and Dawn on the 'Frog Camp' at Leeds in 1983.

The Price Family

The chavies playin'.
(Romanes)

Sonny was holding the head of the black mare. We were walking it for a drink.

We were stopping on a camp up the York Road in Leeds with all the family in 1985.

We were all stoppin' together with me Mam and Dad and all the family on a big ground in Leeds.

This is Kevin's trailer with Dougie Boy on the three wheeler Honda and Me, Sonny, Kacks and Bullerman sat on the step.

...children playing

We 'ad Kushti times.
(Romanes)

This is me with me cousins, Mags, Kacks and Fi lookin' after me brother, Bullerman.

We were camping in the middle of Leeds on a piece of old ground in Hunslet.

We were playing up and down and it was good times when we were all little.

This was back in 1988.

This is Elvis and Margaret's trailer on the same camp in Hunslet in 1988.

Young Bobby Lee

My name's Robert Lee Junior. I was born 18th November 1956. I suppose my life's been different to most Travellers that's been fetched up in trailers, such as me Dad.

...tells his story

Older Travellers didn't really get settled down in school, did they? They go to one school, then they move on and go to another one. I mean, he can read and write, me Dad like, but he didn't really get a good education. So that's why he made sure we did. He wanted us to have a good education.

I went right through school. It's a good thing, I suppose. I can read and write. A lot of Travellers can't. But I think they learn you a lot of things at school that you don't really need to learn, such as science and chemistry and all that, because I can't see what good that's gonna do you through life. If you're not going to be a physician or whatever they are.

I left school then at fifteen years old. Then I went with my Uncle Billy then, when I left school. I went working with him on the scrap and what have you. And I lived with him for a while. Then I came back home. But I've always been with Travellers, like.

It doesn't really matter to me. I mix with a lot of Gorgio people and I like 'em, and I've got a load of friends that's Gorgio people and I've got a load of friends that's Travelling people, and I can't really see any difference. Just how they've been fetched up different. They know I'm a Traveller.

I'm a 'Romany Traveller'. But all the people I drink with, a lot of Gorgio people that I drink with, I go in the Cherry Tree a lot, they all know what I am, and they just treat you the same as anybody else. Which I suppose a lot of people do.

A lot of people don't treat Travellers the same because - people who don't treat them how they should, they just don't understand them, do they, what they are. A lot of people call them 'mucky' and 'scruffy' and such as this, but I suppose if they invited them into their homes, they'd see that they're not.

I think there is prejudice against Travellers. I've heard people talking about Travellers and that, and I suppose sometimes they've got a right when they - I don't know - such as these can't play on the football field, that was full of rubbish, trees tipped and all that, and I suppose they get the wrong opinion. We haven't been fetched up like that. My Dad always said, when they had to move on to another place, his Mother and Father made sure that they picked everything up that was about. He said you couldn't pick a matchstick up where they'd been. Where they'd had the fire, they used to go and dig a bit of turf up and cover it. That's what I've been told.

I think life on the road's finished now. It's all fights and that now, isn't it? It's not like it used to be when my Dad was a kid. But you still get all the stories and that, and I like to sit and listen to 'em. My Dad's Uncle used to tell a good tale. It's a pity he's not here now - he's dead now, old Eddie Smith - he was a lot older than me - I was only fourteen or fifteen - but I could sit and listen to him all night.

I've learned Romany, the biggest part of it, but it's not used at all now, really, just odds and ends and bits and bats. I don't think it's used a lot now, and I think a lot of Travellers, young Travellers today, don't really know it, because I think it's a thing of the past now. Like, me Dad knows it, he knows a lot of it, and he learnt me. Obviously I don't know a great deal, but I know if he says something to me, I know what he's on about. Like he might do if we're out somewhere, trying to buy some'at or he'll say some'at, and the people you're talking to don't know what you're on about, but I do, and he's telling me that and I know.

This is my Aunt Dinah, aged about twenty. It was taken in Leeds in the 1940's.

This is me and Ricky James and Trevor Smith. We were up at Appleby having a look around.

This was taken on the Roman Road, where they sell the horses, back in 1987.

I just think it's a good thing to write a book about Travellers. To educate people about 'em, just to let 'em know what they *are* like.

There is a lot of prejudice, isn't there? There's a lot of prejudice against all races, I suppose, like the blacks and all that, and people don't understand them do they, like they don't understand Travellers. People that don't understand 'em should really spend a day with 'em and see what they're like.

Yes, what I've learned about Travellers I've got off me Dad and that. I used to go stop with me Granny, as well, me Dad's Mother. Six week holiday again. I used to go stop with her in t'trailer in Domestic Street, and what have yer. I think that's how I got to know the biggest part of t'Travellers over there, when I were with me Granny, 'cos there were always trailers about, eight or nine of 'em stopping together.

Then you'd start palling about with the children, and you just get to know 'em, and you grow up with 'em, and they're good friends is Travellers.

I'd like to trace our family history. I don't know whether it's the Library where you go, to go back to me Dad's family, you know, his father and his father and his father. But you can, can't yer, if you go to a certain place, you know to go real well back. Whether it's 1700's or what have you. I've always said that I'd love to do that, go right back, on my Dad's side, the Lees, and just go right back to his father and his father, and to see where you originate from.

My Grandad was a Bobby Lee. His father I think it was John Inan, or just Inan. And his mother was Nancy. 'Cos they were two Lees. You see me Grandad's mother and father were both Lees. I think they come from up north, Stockton, Middlesbrough way.

I don't think the Welsh Lees, and London Lees are any relation to us, though. I don't think so anyway. But you have relations all over t'country that you don't even know.

You go down to Birmingham or somewhere and you start talking to people, and next think you know, they're great-grandmother was your great-grandmother, and you find out that you're related along the line. But he were a horse dealer, my Grandad. That's all he did, horses and that. He was really dedicated on his horses.

I've got two daughters there that I'll tell 'em where they come from, and try and learn them a little bit of Romanes and what have you. But I think that side of it's finished. You don't hear 'em talk Romanes now, as I say, just odds and ends when you're out. Like my Dad says, when he were younger, he used to talk it all t'time. Him and Billy Wharton could have a conversation in Romanes.

I've only met foreign Travellers at such as Spain and that. Some of 'em speaks a mixture of our language, you know, of Romanes. You can talk to them, they'll say *"You've a cushty gad on"*. Gad, shirt, a good shirt, like. And in Germany, our Twinny said, before she died (she were over there, she come back badly) she said they spoke a bit of broken Romanes, English Romanes. German Romanichals, like. Remember that documentary when they had the Gypsies in Concentration Camps and that?

They reckoned that they killed as many Gypsies as they did Jews. They did a documentary on the Gypsies that were in Concentration Camps. They were talking to 'em and we picked up a load, and they were saying that she knew it were her son because she seen his 'gad'. And little bits you could pick out.

Biggest part of them, if you got in with 'em, you'd pick the language up, because you'd be able to talk to one another in broken Romanes - like when you go abroad, you talk in broken English - you'd probably make out in Romanes. Some Indians do, annorl. When I've been for an Indian meal in a restaurant, they call water *'pani'*, they call it 'pani' as well. And five - number five, they call it *'panche'*.

Some think Gypsies come from Egypt. It said in the beginning they were cast to the four corners of the earth, of the world. Some went that way, this way and this way, and they come from every corner of the globe. My uncle Bob said they come from India, way back.

This is me brother Andrew, with me sisters Christine and our Helen together with me mother Pat and me.

We were just havin' a drink in the Cross Green pub in 1987, before Andrew went back over to America.

This is a twelve month old Saluki cross Greyhound Lurcher dog, which I've just bought and hope it will do well.

It's a good shaped, good lookin' dog - but looks don't kill hares!

I started off coursing - it were me Dad's brother that got me into coursing, my Uncle Billy. He's dead now, God rest his soul. I was about ten year old and I used to go, he were stopping at Wetherby then on the waterside, in a trailer, and in the six weeks school holidays, 'cos me Dad made us go to school, you see. In the six weeks school holidays I always used to go and stop with him for the six weeks, and they had lurchers then, and I used to get up on a morning and take his dogs off, and that's how I got into coursing.

Well, if you've got a good dog you can have a bet on it. It just depends how much you've got or how much you want to bet for. They can bet for hundreds, they can bet for thousands. It depends how wealthy you are, I suppose, and how good your dog is. But you just go - big flat fields is best really - 'cos generally, if you have a match on, there's generally twenty people there. Like if I had a match with somebody, like Mick Smith would come and Ricky and Sammy James and all them would come and watch me. Say if I were matching there, in Stokesley called Dicky Dido and he had maybe ten or twelve with him, but all friends like who know each other. You just all walk the fields and say you've got first hare, like, if it jumps up, you don't have to slip your dog, if you think the hare's too far away, you don't have to slip it, if you're running for money, you can hold it up till it's close enough for you to slip off. 'Cos there's a lot of woods and that around. Once they gets into woods it's very rare your dog kills in them - they've lost 'em, you know. They live on the ground, they don't burrow, and all you look for - your best thing when your coursing is you walk through the fields, you've got your dog on a slip lead, and you've just got to look around, and you can see 'em. If they see you coming they just lay flat. You've got to keep your eye on 'em, 'cos when you see 'em, you're running towards them with your dog, you just see a little mound of muck where they've dug the seat out, and then you can see their backs - a little brown bit.

When they hear you coming, they get right flat to the floor, and if you take your eye off 'em, I've run to 'em - I've seen it sat and I've known it's there, and I've run to it with me dog, and I've looked over somewhere else and I've looked back, and I just can't see it. They've gone, you know, they're flat to the floor. Walked all round where I've seen it, and then all of a sudden, you'll just look down and it'll be there at the side of you. Yes, I've walked past loads of 'em. I've walked past 'em and carried on walking, and somebody's shouted and you look behind you, and they've jumped up behind you. You know, they've layed that still and flat, you just can't see 'em.

But it's a good sport, and it's not cruel, I think, because you've got one dog and one hare, you see. More hares get away than get killed, because they're very fast. It depends how good the dog is and how good the hare is. A matter of minutes, really, five minutes is a long race. But you get some dogs, you get bad dogs. You can get a fast dog and they'll be all over 'em, 'cos your hare's ducking and diving all the time; it doesn't stay in front of it, the hare, when your dog's behind it. It's eyes are there, and it sees at back of it, so when your dog's like that and it goes down to pick it up, it ducks out o't'way, and your dog's turning every other way, and there's dogs that won't pick 'em up, I think they're too frightened to throw themselves at 'em and

pick 'em up. Striking they call it. But if you get a good striker, as soon as they get behind 'em and start messing 'em about, they just pick 'em up. Yes. Well, they don't kill them straight away, but once they've picked 'em up, they sort of hold 'em down for a while, a matter of a minute or so and they're dead, you know. Canine teeth are like that, and they just go straight through the chest, and they kill 'em. Biggest part of 'em carry them back to you then. You can see 'em carrying the hare back to you. I run with 'em, the dogs, and see all the race, that's why you're better off on big flat fields, because you can see all the race then. If it's hilly, they've only go to go over a hill and you don't see any of the race.

Whoever kills most hares wins the bet. Yes. I've got three, you've got three. We all walk into a field, you've got your dog on a slip, I've got my dog on a slip. You spin a coin maybe, or say "Do you want first hare? I'll have first hare", or whatever. So you all start walking the field, so say it's my first hare, if a hare jumps up and I think it's right enough, if it's not close to a wood or owt, you know, 'cos you're just throwing your money away that way. If it's close to a wood, they're straight into the wood, it's very rare a dog kills 'em in a wood. And if I think it's going to be a good slip or anything, it's got a chance of killing it, I'll slip it, so if mine it's first hare, then your kills yours, and then it depends on you then, how you want to go. If you kill three and I kill three, you should just call it a draw, and that's all well and done, or you can add another hare on, have another hare, till the first one that misses. Oh yes, sometimes you can walk on and there's twenty hares on it, in one big field. Sometimes you can walk on and there's two or three. That's why you keep going to different places all the time, to find where there's more hares.

It's not illegal, no. They're trying to ban all blood sports now, aren't they, foxing and all such as that, but it's not illegal, but what it is - you're trespassing, you see. That's what's illegal about it. You're going on to somebody's land, you see, and trespassing. Because obviously farmers have shoots and that, and they charge people to come onto their land and shoot game, don't they? So you're killing three or four hares off their land what they probably can sell, I don't know. But on the other hand, they're moaning about them eating all the crops. At least when a dog gets hold of a hare it kills it. Some of these men that shoot 'em, they're laying or crawl away, and they suffer more, you see. They die in agony, don't they? But it's a good sport. I like it me. And my Dad used to go years ago, but he doesn't bother now.

This was the last photograph I had taken with me Dad, in 1998 when this book was being made.

Our John is playing and laughing around with his older cousins, Heather, the twins, Elijah and Arthur and Margaret Kindon. There's our 'Morecambe' trailer in the background.

This was near the wash house in Holbeck, Hainsworth's Yard in 1963. It belonged to Showpeople and old Mrs. Morley let us stop in the yard, as we had nowhere else to go.

There was no sites in those days.   Ada North

There were many camps in Leeds in the early sixties.

We got stoppin' on bits of grounds when they knocked the houses down.

There were no facilities back then and no sites.

This is Jim and Dorothy Price and their family camping on some waste ground which was in Armley, Leeds.

Tommy Doherty

HOLBECK and ARMLEY

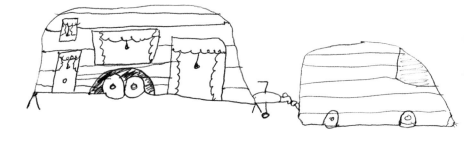

HUNSLET, LEEDS IN THE LATE SIXTIES

We were camping on here for about six months. There was us, the Dorans, Tom Connors and all his family, Old Joe Moloney and his family, some of the Brazils, and the Morrisons. We used to have some great old songs round the fire. There were no facilities, you had to collect water from the neighbours in the houses, people didn't mind back then. It was an old site where they had pulled down houses and was very mucky. Eventually we got moved off and found another camp and pulled in, there was a lot of demolition then. They were pulling Leeds down!

Bill Doran

HUNSLET

Leeds Eviction 1968

TOMMY DOHERTY'S REMINISCENCES

EVICTION 1968

The Council Landrover was used by the Eviction Officer to tow the trailers off the land onto the road. The police would then compound the trailers for parking on the highway.

We put children into the trailers and pointed out to the police that the council was breaking the law, as it is illegal to tow a trailer with people inside.

We also put Travellers on the tow bar and underneath the back axle to stop them towing the trailers onto the road.

The Travellers stuck together and this went on for two years.

After these two years, Leeds City Council realised they were losing the battle and invited us to a meeting to set up a site on a temporary basis. That's the permanent site now at Cottingley Springs.

...from Holbeck camp

EVICTION 1968

That was the first trailer we ever had – we had just come out of the wagons.

We sold the wagons in Barnsley and got that trailer out. This was in 1968.

There's me, me brother Kevin, me old Dad and the babies were in the trailer. We were sat there to stop them hooking up the trailer with the council Landrover and pulling us off the ground.

That's Tommy Doherty arguing with the Council man, telling him he can't shift us.

It was a close community then, everyone stuck together and helped each other.

Leeds Eviction 1968

EVICTION 1968

This is our trailer with all Fred's children on it - me Dad's brother's family.

They are sitting on the towing bar to stop them pulling us off. It was the only way to get stopping in those days.

There were no sites and nowhere to go.

This is me old Dad, me and me brother Dougie trying to get stopping.

...tryin' to get stoppin'

RIGHTEOUS PRICE'S REMINISCENCES

Sakie Lee

My name's Sakie Lee. I was born a Gypsy, in a trailer all my life. The only part when I wasn't in a trailer was when I was born in Hospital at Southampton.

...in his own words

Well they pulled in from London, from one part of central London to have me in Southampton. We was on a site for four years at Southampton. We used to travel a little bit in the summer and then come back to the site in the winter. I was the eldest of my family. The eldest of seven. There's another boy and there's five girls. I can go back a long ways. I can remember my poor old grandmother. She was a very good woman, she used to tell me like old stories about the olden days. My Granny was named Miranda Price but she married a Lee man, so that made her a Lee. She was born in Wales, brought up in Wales, and she travelled Ireland, she travelled all over, my Granny did, all over Ireland, all over England, and all over the counties, you know. My Grandad was named Nelson Lee.

They could speak Romany fluent. Deep Romany - the real old stuff. I never did see my Grandad - he was passed on before I was even born. But I did see a lot of my Granny - a lot. She was, stopping with us in Southampton, and she also used to travel along with us when we used to move in the summer times.

I've been to Appleby. I've been to Epsom, Epsom Downs. I've been to Newcastle Town Moor. I've been to Barnet (that's a fair that's done away with now, by the way), and I've been to a lot of Scotch fairs, but knowing the name of 'em, I just couldn't say off-hand.

We just used to pull on and mostly me Dad would like a drink. So he'd go to the Public in the night and sometimes in the day, while we were just left to make our own sport up, you know, amongst all our own people. We'd like spinning - spinning the coins up - or we'd like gambling with cards or bits of things like that, or riding the horses.

It's very hard on the road, there's not much travelling in England these days. Not much travelling in England at all. The law is very strict, they've brought new rules out and it's very hard. They can also confiscate your caravan off you, and things like that you know, if you don't move when they say move.

In one way it's getting better, 'cos there's caravan sites made and also the Council will give you a house today. They never used to think of such a thing for Gypsies - always used to move us on, give us no say like. I think my Mam'll end up in a house one of these days, my Mam, 'cos she's waiting now - she's bought a piece of ground, like, and they won't pass her for the licence, so the Council came down, they said *"Mrs Lee if we have to shift you from this place, we might have to give you a house. Would that be alright with you?"* My mother said *"That'll be fine"*, and my father said *"It'll be fine."*

There was this one time - it was at Peckham, London - and the policeman came to move us, but we asked them, could we have 'til morning, because it was very late in the night when they came. What happened was, the policeman gave us 'til morning, but there were some kids, some young kids, come pelting us with stones, so we had to move on very late in the night. It was very hard them days.

We used to travel a lot up Scotland, around Aberdeen, Glasgow and that way, and we used to travel also Caernarfon in Wales, around them places like, you know, there's stopping places there, and a lot in London. Traditional places, old places like, that we used to go to. We'd stop with family. Mostly my Granny's family. And sometimes we'd stop with my other Grandfather and Granny. His name was Fred Lee and my Granny was named Ash Elder Lee. Ash Elder Price was her single name, but she married a Lee so that made her a Lee - Ash Elder Lee. There wouldn't be many of us; sometimes there might be two families, sometimes there would be one family. We'd pull in with the other caravans, even though

Duvers mandi and me puri dai

(Romanes)

GRANDMUM AND SAKIE *Miranda Lee and Sakie.*

they'd be complete strangers to us; we'd all get on as one. Them days it was a lot easier; there was no such things as burgling one another them days. But today you've got to watch who you pull in with. They were a lot closer.

Like, say the women went out together and one never took bread money - the other one would hand her some bread money, who'd done good like that day, you know. And therefore the men used to do a bit of scrapping, in the modern times. A bit of scrapping metals and rags. So one fellow never done good, another would help him out as well. Yes, that was the way - the way of those times. Some days you'd be up and some days you'd be down.

It's a lot better life today. Things is more easier - it's more convenient. These caravan sites they're beautiful to stop on, if you get the peace and quiet. You've got water, you got a bathroom, you've got all the conveniences. You can go and do what you want. If you wanted to move out for a couple of weeks you could, to go to a fair or anything like that. There'd be no questions asked.

The old days you were always on the move, always. If you had a week in one place, you'd be very fortunate. Two weeks was amazing, like, you'd get used to the surroundings and you'd want to stay there, but you realised that you couldn't - when the law came to move you on, you had to go. All of the time.

All the policemen used to shift us. From all different parts of the country - from Wales, from London, from Scotland, from Manchester, from Leeds, you name it they used to shift us.

The law was very civil. Always got to hand 'em 'em's due - very good people and I agree with the work that they're doing. I like them very much. But even though, there's some of the lads would get up to a little bit of mischief, like. I couldn't say what they do, nor nothing like that, but they don't like them so much - they gives 'em bad names. But there's got to be a reason for the law and the law is doing a good job.

No, I wouldn't like to live in a wagon - no. Times'd be too hard, and they'd be too cold. Maybe if I was born to it, maybe I would have like it then, but no, not now, I wouldn't like to go into one. My Mother and my Father was born in wagons, yes. They never said too much about wagons. My poor old grandma used to be the one who'd give me information about the wagons. She said times used to be very hard my boy. You might have a trade for a wagon off a feller, a strange feller, and you might go in and you might find (God'll forgive me for saying this) like bugs in it. And then you'd have to burn the whole thing. Start with the wheels and build it up again, the old men used to do, when they was like that, build them up from the shafts on the wheels.

The main stop was in Wales. Around the Rhonda valleys and valley docks was the stopping place them days. That'd be anywhere where there would be grass. It might be along the roadside, it might be in a field, wherever they could put the horses to the grass, that's where they'd tether them. It was all open camps. No such thing as a caravan site. You'd just pull in. You were allowed maybe two or three days on each place. Lucky to get a week them days. But I suppose in Ireland, it was real good in Ireland. They'd let you stop in one place as long as you liked in Ireland. They were used to the Travellers.

I love horses, yes, but I haven't got me horses myself. Me Dad and Mam don't bother with horses. The last horse we had when I was about seven year-old, was an old grey horse and I tell you that wasn't much cop. It'd cut you down as soon as look at you, you know. It was only a young 'un, but I didn't like it. And ever since then I didn't really bother with horses. But now me uncle's got about seventeen or eighteen on the caravan site in Wakefield, and they're quite nice - they're easy to get on with - they don't cut you down nor nothing - they're just good horses. Keeping horses is just something that went on from years and centuries. You don't need to learn to ride - you just jump on and you're away.

Travelling was to gain a living. It would get very thin for my Mam's kind of work, you know, fortune-telling and hawking and things like that. She'd hawk lace. Lace, charms and now, up to about three years ago, she used to hawk tablecloths. Years ago it was flowers and pegs. The men used to do trade with the horses to keep the family going - like sell horses, deal in horses, but the women, once the men made the pegs and flowers, the women used to go out and sell them.

When peg-making, they used to have a knife called a peg knife - that was a knife cut out of a tree, carved down into the handle and they used to shove a blade into it. If you wanted a flower knife it would need to be thin, very thin, to carve the flowers out. But if you wanted a peg knife it needed to be a thick-bladed knife, so you could turn the pegs and split them down the middle. There was ash and there was willow and there was nut, nut tree. And for flowers there was elderberry and willow.

When flower-making, well, they'd just hold the knife on em's knee, and they'd just sort of carve along, carve very gently and very slowly (there's a knack to it), and the flower would curl, it would keep curling, they'd keep going, keep going 'til the stick wear down thin, and then when it was thinnest, the stick would just crack off and the flower would be made. Then they pushed a little sort of twig in it, to hold it up like a flower, and they dyed them in a flower dye, to colour them. All different colours: orange, yellow, all the colours, red. My aunts used to make paper flowers. That was no problem to them.

Moho Grandad is kellin' his hobin around an old stick fire. Suzie is kalarvin' the dish out.

(Romanes)

Grandad and me Aunt Suzie.

My granny had three daughters that used to go out hawking, or calling. But now they've had to stop, because they're getting on the old side. There's only two of them left now - two of the girls. My granny passed on about thirteen years ago. I think the youngest one of my aunts would be about seventy, so you can see the point of view - they had to give it up. They're all on old-age pension now. They used to do fortune-telling, like, you know, they used to do duckerin'. It's a thing that would be handed down from centuries and centuries. God knows where it came from. My granny could tell fortunes, and also my aunts could and my Mam can. Well not now, 'cos she's living off the dole, like, you know. She's give it all up. My sisters didn't want to know nothing. My Mam tried to pass it on but they married young and they didn't seem to want to know.

I've done a lot of farmwork. Done a lot of fruit picking, potato picking, plum picking, apple picking, all things like that, hop picking. In the country.

It's very important, the family, to Travellers. Some parents are very strict. But my mother and father, no, they wasn't strict at all. They let me sisters and me brother or me get married any time I'd choose to. Or any of us. The girls have to buckle down a bit. They're quite looked after, they are. Like they're not allowed to go astray or anything like that. They're not allowed to make a mistake with a man. No they ain't. They take one man and they stick to one man.

I think things will change there again. I do honestly. I can't put me finger right on it, but it's just the way things goes, isn't it? There's a lot into the television. It's showing you lots of kissing and cuddling and where it never used to do, you know, on television. It'd just be comedies at one time. I quite like television, I do. It'd be boring without it. I like 'Neighbours', I like old cowboy films, old sword fencing films, I like. And old Johnny Weismuller films, 'Tarzan'. He's quite good - he's a very good swimmer. Yes, I'm glad of television. I would not prefer to go back to the old days, no.

They all married one another, like the Prices married the Lees and the Lees married the Prices, and except for Lees and Prices, they might marry into a Boswell, or a Smith. As for the rest, no. Just the Smiths, the Lees, the Prices and another name again, the Joneses, they was always one, considered as the one family, like they could all talk one another's language in the old days, and they were considered as the same sort of family. All of these names that I've named is Welsh Gypsies.

In the old days they were arranged marriages. It was just done like the Indians is today, and the Pakistans. They'd find a nice feller, one amongst the tribe, and they'd say *"Daughter, there's a nice man, if you can see it in your heart to get coupled up with this feller, we'd consider it as an honour as you'd go and get married."* That's the way it was done.

Well them days, I should be ashamed to say this, we didn't have Church weddings, we didn't have Register Office weddings. The feller just took the girl, and lived with her for one night, and that was considered married for the rest of them's life. That was in my Mam and Dad's day. My Mam and Dad's also married that way. Not a Church wedding.

It was called 'jumping the broomstick', them days. That's going back centuries ago though, - like to the slave days, when the Gypsies and the poor black people was considered as slaves. Then they used to jump the broomstick to get married. That's the truth. Some of our people used to tie 'ems hands together with a band, in the real olden days, I mean centuries ago now, and they'd say a few words to one another, like: *"I'll take you if you'll take me"*, *"Yes"*, they'd say, *"I'll take yer"*, and they'd be married like that way.

That was in private amongst them's own selves. Them two selves. Nobody would be around, just them

two. And then they'd come back and let all the family know that they were married. The gal would get a dowry. It all depends on the times. Like, them years ago what we're talking about now, one hundred sovereigns would be a lot of money. So that's what they'd get.

That was in my poor Grandad and Granny's days. It would be give to my Granny, to start her off. But if like my Grandad wanted something, she'd have to give it to him without any questions asked. It was my Grandad. He was the boss. That was always the way. The old man used to run the home. Women used to do the fortune-telling and things like that, but the men was always the boss. What the men said, that was law. All up to the man. The women would look after the money. They'd look after it and then it would be handed to the men, without any questions at all asked. It'd be handed in em's hand.

Me sisters' weddings, they were quite big but they were in Register Offices, and my brother's also was in a Register Office - that wasn't very big. My father was there, my mother was there, my brother's wife was there, my brother was there. That was about all that was in that wedding because they runned away together, you see, without the girl's mother and father knowing about it. They done a runner, so they had no time to get together. But once you're married, that's all, they can't do nothing about it, you see.

Her people, after they were married, then they considered them as the family. They were took right in. The poor old woman she was called Cheeky Nicholson. She was a very polite woman. She loved me brother. She treated him as her own son. She was a good woman.

I'm a Christian. I wasn't brought up a Christian. I've been a Christian now for about eight or nine years. I went to a Christian meeting at Wakefield - it was in a tent - and they preached to me that strong, I decided I had to become one. It was a fellow called David Jones. He is a Gypsy man.

Well, in foreign countries the Gypsies have been Christians for a long time, but in this country it's just starting to get around to the people now today. He put the fear of God into me, I had to become a Christian. The words was like fire coming - real strong stuff, you know. If you would have listened, I think you would have changed as well, if you would have heard that man preach.

I am glad I became a Christian. I don't swear so much. I hardly swear at all, as a matter of fact. And I tries to keep meself quiet, I don't bother with any other people, I don't get no arguments or anything like that. So it has, it has made a big change in my life.

I'd do anything what would come into me mind before, anything. And I used to like fights a lot. I used to be fighting all the time. First two pints of beer, I'd be battling. If anybody said one word out of place - anybody. That's changed - through the Christianity. I'd just stop and walk away from them now. It's a lot easier and simpler, and a lot happier. It's more easier, more easier than a busted nose or a busted mouth. All you've got to do is get up and walk away. But mind you, if they did keep on too far, if they wouldn't let me go, then you'd have to fight and do the best you could. You'd be forced into doing it then, like an eye for an eye sort of thing, you know. But I just prefer to go and leave it.

Funerals - very sad times. As many as possible would be at a funeral - all of the families. Quite big - funerals. They'd come from all over, maybe London, Wales, all over the place. When there was somebody died in the wagon - in the wagon - then they'd burn it. At the time that was the only thing to do, that was the way of life. But if they died outside the wagon, then they'd sell it. But like I say, that is sort of dying out today, as well. I've seen it done once amongst our people lately. They always had pieces of jewellery; brooches, neck chains, bangles, rings. That would get broke and burnt. And also the pots, the cans, everything what was inside the caravan would be burnt. Maybe thousands of pounds worth of stuff. It

It's me, the chavi, holding hands with me Granny atchin' on the atchin' tan.
The zumin angras are hanging on the kettle iron over the yog.

(Romanes)

Me and me Grannie Miranda stopping on a camp.

would still be burnt. Now it's all changed with our families. Now the thing what is done today, if somebody passed on in a trailer, the first thing we'd want to do is get rid of that trailer - perhaps sell it - straight away - not own it, no more.

Travellers dressed in plaid shirts and all that - they liked bright colours, handkerchiefs. That was done in the old days. There's still some amongst us now what does it. Not today, it's all modern times today, denim jeans and all that.

They buy Crown Derby and Worcester. Just because they're bright colours, and it looks fancy when they're put up in the trailers. There's no other reason for it. And they like jewellery, a lot of our people, like bracelets, neck chains and rings. Happen that's just from the old days as well. I think that started from India.

There was old songs, but honestly they've well gone out of me head, and me poor old Granny used to sing 'em regular, as well. Like Welsh songs they was, real old. Unaccompanied, just without music. She was a good old singer. And you won't believe this, but who was my Granny's favourite singer, when she was a woman about near enough a hundred when she died? - Elvis Presley. Yes, she really liked Elvis Presley. And she said her poor old Grandad, he was called Chasey Price - he used to sing like Slim Whitman - and do the yodel. When she heard Slim Whitman singing a sad song, tears would come in her poor old eyes, 'cos it'd put her in mind of her grandfather.

Well, I've got an uncle called Blacky, he's only a youngish fellow, about 40-odd - he strums on the guitar, but he's not all that good. There was a man called William Lee. He used to play a fiddle, really in the old days though. In my uncle's and aunt's days. He was quite good on the box, he was a good player. They'd have Gypsy tunes, and also Welsh. And some Scottish tunes amongst them. It has gone now. From our type of people. But there's still the Gypsies over in Spain what believes in music - the guitar, the fiddle, and you know. They believes in music. They are, beautiful players. Very nice people.

I never had no schooling. Always on the travel. I had no schooling at all. My sisters had a bit of schooling. It was mostly in Southampton. There's my sister June; she's quite a good reader now. And my sister Suzanne can make a few words up. My poor sister Shirley - I don't think she can read at all now. She had no schooling. And my brother Peter's got a wife who can read and write, and he can pick the odd signs up. They said it was very hard with the house people - very hard getting on with them - you couldn't mix. They were picked on a lot, being Gypsies like. They had to put up with it. That was the way it was.

I never went to school at all. The only bit of schooling I done was trying to learn to read and write lately. And I think I left it a bit too late. If I had to live over again and know what I know now, I would have made sure that me Mam got somewhere where she could have settled and given me a bit of schooling, even if it would have been for four or five years. Because we did stay in that place, like I say, Southampton, four or five years in the winter, and we would have had enough time, but I just didn't realise at the time. I wanted to be like me Dad and Mam was, unschooled.

Your mind changes as you get older - you seem to realise right from wrong, you know. And it was wrong not going to school - I think so. They didn't think it was wrong. They still don't think of it - they say *"You can read, or you can't read"*. But even though they consider my Anna a blessing amongst the family, 'cos she can read and write like a good 'un, like, you know. She reads all the papers and all the bits of forms - she fills 'em in for 'em, so she's a real blessing in the family - a great help, yes.

Mixing with non-Travellers - that was a thing that wasn't done. Now we might play in a playground and some of the non-Travellers might come and try to mix with us, but instead of trying to mix with us as friends, they'd mix up like *"Do you want a fight?"* and things like that there, you know, so we didn't mix much with them. That was all the way up 'til I was about seventeen or eighteen, then things started to change, then I was getting friends amongst those people, I was getting good friends amongst them, 'cos I have got quite a lot of good friends amongst those people. You know when you were young you could not mix, 'cos they'd all want to fight or they'd pelt you with stones, or sometimes worse. They were really hard, yes. It's just, when you wear the name 'Gypsy', a house fellow or a house lady they just don't want to know.

The students, they're really interested. I quite like them, as well. A lot of the colleges - they're very nice. As a matter of fact, I didn't expect them to be that way, so understanding like, but it's the new ones coming up today - like they let live, you know, they let people go on the way they wants to go - but the old people, they're strictly in their own way. Do you know what I mean? And if you're not in their way, you're considered as an outsider.

I want my daughter to go to a good school. I do, yes. And I want her to have a nice job, so she can look after herself. I don't want none of their money. I don't want nothing belongs to her - if anything I'm going to supply the clothes and everything that she needs, like. Just as long as she can get a job to keep herself going, like might even save up for a car for herself when she's older and things like that, you know. And if she gets married, of course I'll pay for the wedding, and things like that, and I'll be happy to get rid of her one time.

I'd like her to get a job. Yes, I'd say *"Go ahead"*, I would. Even a policewoman, I'd say, *"Go ahead"*. Yes, indeed I would. The days have changed. Yes, I do feel that. Even if she wanted to marry a country bloke - like a house feller, I'd say, *"If you love him, my girl, and he's good to you"*, I'd say, *"you go ahead."* In the older days it just wasn't done.

❁

Well, I'm thirty-three, coming thirty-four at the moment. It's old enough. I'm putting my mark down. I've done about everything there is to do. I've done everything. I know all about the Gypsy life, I know everything about it, I've done it all. The only thing I haven't done is lived in a horse-drawn wagon. Everything except for that, I've done it.

Sooner or later now, I don't know how soon or how much later, I think I'm going to take a house myself. For my Anna's sake. My little baby's sake. She'd get a better schooling, and she'd be treated more better in a house that what she would on the road, like in a caravan. That's my opinion, but there's others what got different opinions.

❁

The site, it's quite nice. The only thing where it could be a little bit better, then, maybe if there wasn't so many so close up again' us. But look, my neighbour, he's never there and this people's quite a way from us, so really we're in a good place ain't we? We're in one of the nicest parts on this ground, I think so.

If my mother and father got their ground passed, I'd sooner be stopping there meself, because not only is it a nicer place, it would be a lot nicer, because they would have it concreted and all things like that - tarmaced out, you know, and also I wouldn't mind being so far from me Mam. Like this isn't too far away - I can go and see her when I want. But if that place was passed, I think I would go back again to have my own piece of ground. But this is good enough, but like I say, if I had me choice and it got passed and everything got done proper, I'd sooner be there. I'm living quite a reasonable life.

Topcliffe Charter Fair

TOPLEY FAIR

'The fields on the edge of the town Thirskwards were filled with encampments, the tents, waggons, vans and carts of potters, tinkers and gypsies. During the fair, free fights were continually in progress down Mill Lane, and it was very generally understood that every quarrel which occurred during the year, no matter how trivial, had to be settled off with a stand up fight at Topley Fair. It was a long-standing custom and died hard. Even the women-folk in those good old days had also their 'arena' or place of tournament for fisticuffs; the latter was a plot of land, to the left, across the bridge.'

'Richmondshire and the Vale of Mowbray' by Edmund Bogg (1906)

CAMPING AT TOPCLIFFE, 1904

'The families pulled on to the field by the river and an encampment developed, before, during and after the fair.'

Thirsk Museum

There were three fields to stop in at Topley Fair. This is the first field and they'd be settlin' down here to have the horse trading. You can see all the washing thrown on the hedges and bits of line. They used to do it all by hand in tubs or baths. There was no chrome cans in those days. They were galvanised cans with brass rims around them and painted different colours.

Ada Kendal

GYPSIES ON THE MOVE, 1906

'A curious crowd has gathered to watch these tented carts move their way through Westgate in Thirsk, on their way to camp at Topcliffe Fair.

They are thought to be Hungarian Gypsies or from elsewhere in Eastern Europe.'

'Around Thirsk-Britain in Old Photographs' by Cooper Harding and Peter Wyon (1995)

These are wagons with accomodations on. They are making their way from the North to, go through Thirsk on the way to Topley Fair.

Tom Kendal

- known as 'Topley'

TOPLEY TRADITIONS

'...In the days of our fathers, Topcliffe Fair (locally called 'Topley'), 17th and 18th July, was one of the most important in the North of England, both for horses, sheep and nearly all manner of merchandise; and on the days of the fair any person could procure a license for selling beer by displaying a green bush or branch at his door. And so drinking booths were erected at every lane end leading towards Topcliffe for three miles around, so that folks travelling to the fair were able to quench their thirst, not only at the fair, but in their coming and returning also. For instance, a booth was erected at Norton le Clay, one at Dishforth, one at Rainton and Aisenby, etc., and every village around reared its refreshment saloon on this auspicious occasion.' 'Richmondshire and the Vale of Mowbray' by Edmund Bogg (1906)

THE FAIRGROUND RIDES AT TOPCLIFFE FAIR, 1904
'These can be seen here, in the field by the bridge across the river.' Thirsk Museum

THE FAIRGROUND AT TOPCLIFFE FAIR, TAKEN FROM THE CHURCH TOWER, 1930's

Topcliffe Charter Fair

A TRADITIONAL MEETING PLACE

'Topcliffe Fair was granted a Royal Charter in 1343 and was held for hundreds of years until it finally ended in 1970 due to the withdrawal of the charter.

Topcliffe is situated near Thirsk in the North Riding of Yorkshire and had been a popular horse fair for many years. Caravans had been parked beside the River Swale for three days each July with the Gypsies supplying the local farmers with their work horses.

...Topcliffe, like all fairs, was a meeting place where friends and familiies could see each other once a year and swap stories and complete deals...'

'Yorkshire Gypsy Fairs, Customs and Caravans' by E. Alan Jones (1986)

TOPLEY, 1940's

This ws taken in the field at Topley where we all camped for the fair. That's the 'three sisters', me Granny Ryah, Adelina and Vesti, with their mother, old Cinamenti Smith.

Mick Smith

IN A PUBLIC, 1945

That's Uncle Israel, Uncle Arthur and me Dad, Walter in a public. Me Dad had just come out of the army and was having a drink with his brothers.

Mick Smith

ON THE FAIR, 1949

You can see old Cinamenti Smith, me old great-grandmother, smoking a pipe with my cousin Sally and me Aunt Joan. This was taken fifty years ago on the fair.

Mick Smith

TOPLEY TRADITIONS

Topcliffe Fair was a horse dealing Fair and everyone used to meet there on 18th July, the main day, and they'd do the dealing amongst each other. People went every year, it was an annual occasion. It was a North of England Fair, it was on a par with Appleby and it was a great shame for the Fair to end.

My grandfather had the original Charter to the Fair for years and then he gave it to the Parish Priest in Topcliffe for safe keeping and the Fair got done away with.

Mick Smith

This was taken at Topcliffe Fair in the 1950's. It's old Cinamenti Smith, my great grandmother, with her two great granddaughters Doreen and Marie, they are now settled and married in Leeds.

Cinamenti is sat on the Bow top wagon belonging to Isaiah Smith, her son-in-law. She's babysitting the children. She lived to be one hundred and six and used to smoke a clay pipe. She had long plaits of hair right down to her waist. She used to travel all over Yorkshire: Malton, Knottingley, Selby, Leeds and York. She used to go out hawking every day with her big basket selling bits of combs, lace and soaps, her 'swag'.

Isaiah was one of the fastest peg-makers amongst Travellers. He used to make pegs for me Granny to sell and he also sold them to the ironmonger's, 'Scar's', in Leeds Market and Halifax.

I wasn't very old when I used to go to the Fair back in the fifties and I remember looking forward to it every year. We've been to the Fair in Bow top wagons, accomodations, tents and in later years motors and trailers.

Mick Smith

Topcliffe Charter Fair

FAMILY LINKS WITH TOPLEY

UNCLE ISRAEL'S OPEN LOT, 1953

That's me Granny, Riah, JoanAnne Smith and Edna Lee from Huddersfield and my two cousins, the twins, Doreen and Marie.

This was taken outside our open lot wagon which had been made by our Uncle Israel.

Mick Smith

TOPLEY 1955

This is Henry Harker and me, Madge Kindon, before we were married and Hanniball sat on Bob Harker's horse, 'Pride'.

We used to go to Topley every year. We used to pull in the fields by the side of the river. It was all horses and wagons in those days and big square tents like the one at the back.

Madge Harker

GOING TO TOPLEY, 1963

Old Benny and Mary-Ann Smith stoppin' on the roadside before pullin' into Topley field. He was known as 'Old Gypsy Benny' and they always stopped on their own. They've got a Bill Wright's wagon and an open lot. They always went to all the local fairs, Topley, Yarm, Lee Gap, Brough Hill and Appleby. They used to winter around Castleford, over that side.

Ada Kendall

- our family memories

ANNIE BOSWELL REMEMBERS TOPLEY

TOPLEY, 1962

There's our Caroline, 'Moonie' Dear with Kathleen Smith, Lizzy and Mimi Smith with their friends.

All the children were playin' on the field at Topley Fair where we all stopped.

TOPLEY, 1963

Moonie Dear, Mick Dear and Rosalyn Dear - me brother and two sisters. They are stood on the front board of a barrel-top open lot belongin' to me Dad, Alfie Dear.

We were livin' in the wagon and it took us a couple of days to get to Topley Fair, where we pulled in the field.

TOPLEY FAIR, 1964

There's me, Annie Dear and Ambrose, me brother, on Topley Fair with a friend about thirty-five years ago. I was only sixteen and we were stoppin' in the field. It was nice.

We used to be outside singin' round the open fires. We used to go every year. You can see a four-wheeler or dray in the background. This was before I was married.

TOPLEY, 1965

That's me brother, Billy Dear, with one of the Sykes girls, Suzanne Nicholson and Wally Hall on the roadside at Topley in 1965.

That's where we used to pull along there if the field was full up.

The 'Topley' Story Ends

OLD TRADITIONS DIE HARD

HORSE DEALING IN TOPLEY MAIN STREET 1965

The men are standin' around watching the horses go up and down. The horses are tied up waitin' for people to come and buy.

All the dealin' went on in the main street and deals were done with a smack on the hand - 'bargain sealed'.

There were two pubs on the side of the road 'The Angel' and 'The Black Bull' and the men used to go in to have trade, swoppin' horses and dealin' for carts and wagons.

There was a Fish Shop on the corner and you used to go up steps to it.

Around the bend of the road was a bridge and John Jones would play the accordion and they'd do step dances to the tunes on the bridge.

There was an old man who used to sell garden tatties, lettuce, beans and apples out of his house and every year he'd measure all the children and see how they'd grown and mark it on the wall as they'd come to buy.

It was a great Fair and a shame they done away with it. We visited every year, we were part of Topcliffe. Many Gypsies and Travellers were buried at Topcliffe cemetery.

Ada Kendal

'Eighty villagers called a meeting and voted against the fair continuing and the Lord of the Manor, Lord Leconfield agreed to petition the Home Secretary for the withdrawal of the Charter. Thirsk Rural District Council also supported this suggestion and the Topcliffe councillors submitted a proposal to have the fair stopped.'

Yorkshire Gypsy Fairs, Customs and Caravans' by E. Alan Jones (1986)

- who stole The Fair?

THE CASE OF THE GYPSIES AND THE STOLEN FAIR

'The case of the 'stolen Fair' failed to get under way today as nearly thirty Gypsies filled the tiny village courtroom at Wath near Ripon. The Gipsy leader, Mr Tommy Doherty, Chairman of the International Gypsy Council, asked for an adjournment for three weeks so that Gypsies accused of contravening the Highways Act could seek legal advice. The Chairman of the bench, Mr S Alton agreed and adjourned the case until August 10th.'

Yorkshire Evening Post   20.7.1971

For over four hundred years Gypsies from all over the country have flocked to Topcliffe Fair for horse trading. The Royal Charter for the Fair was rescinded and the Fair 'stolen'. The local publican had put an ad in the Times asking for any objections to the Fair being stopped. Not many Gypsies read and no one saw the notice and so no one objected. It was only when everyone came this year that they were told the Fair was done away with. We tried to get it put back on but we couldn't do it, as they had followed the regulations!

It's sad because the Topcliffe Fair legend dates back four hundred years when it is said, Gypsies who were camping by the river saved the life of the Lord of the Manor from drowning. As a gesture of thanks the Lord of the Manor said that the Gypsies could hold a Fair there for one week in July.

Tommy Doherty

These are all Travellers who'd come to try and get stopping at the Fair with Tommy Doherty, when they were trying to do away with the Fair at Topcliffe. There is Black John Tyers, Old Buffer Adams, Keith Anderson, Robert Farrar, Betty Wilson, Rockerbilly, Michael Brough, Laddie Lowther, Billy Foster and Gordon Liversedge.

Peter & Kay James

Shirley Lee

Me Dad was old Fred Lee and me Mother was a Price but she married a Lee, she become a Lee, Ella Lee. All me Mother's children were born at home, every one of eight. I was born in Kingston on Thames in a horse drawn van along the roadside. My father went off to get a nurse and she come down on a bike and brought me into the world.

...telling her own story

I'm a Lee - my father was a Lee. All me other brothers and sisters were registered and christened Lee. My aunt took me away from me Mam and went and had me christened Price. I never did have a birth certificate. Me mother said it got burnt and I can't get a birth certificate. I haven't got no age paper, only I know my age by heart. I'll be fifty-seven on the 10th of this May that's coming. Me Mam told me. I sent my £13 off to Kingston and me money never come back, but they said they can't trace me. 'Cos I wanted to get me pension, how will I get it on time? They call me Shirley, but I'm christened and registered Emily Price and Emily Lee. I should have been registered where I were born; it should have been Kingston, shouldn't it? I've tried to ask me Dad - he's so old he can't remember.

✳

We had two wagons. One caravan was a big one, and my father and mother used to sleep in it. And the other one, it had two beds. Have you seen a bed that goes up and down? Well me and me sister used to lay on the top and me two brothers would lay underneath, but the small children would be underneath the bed in me mother's caravan - the little ones, the small 'uns. It was warm. Lovely. And you'd hear the raindrops on the sheet, on the old green sheet, tip tap, you know.

We loved the horses. My Dad bought all of us a horse apiece. Do you know the horses, the best horses worth so many hundreds now, they were £20 and £30 and £40 apiece. He'd have seven or eight and he'd say, *"That's yours, that's yours, that's yours"*, and give us all a horse apiece. And then after a time he'd sell 'em and change 'em over.

✳

My Mother went to Ireland. My Mother was there a long time - and my husband's people. They liked it. They went over on a boat with their caravans. I don't know how long they was over there. Only I know me Mam used to tell me. Me Mam could tell you a lot. My Father exchanged the old vans, and we got into these kind of trailers. I wasn't very old - about eleven or twelve. These were better. We could get along the road faster, and leave all our troubles behind with the horses. We leave all our worries behind.

We'd get along quicker. Same places, but we'd get along the road faster. And we could park on the car parks in towns, where we'd be in the country with the horses, down the road and down the lane sides and on pieces of waste commons. But we could go anywhere with these. People told us we could park in the car parks in towns, see more of the towns. Lovely, to get in towns, away from the woods and the lanes and the road sides.

✳

I know in London we had a big building ground, named the Old Man's Land. And we used to stay on the common, Chobin Common, Surrey-side, round Kingston. All different places. And Southend. There was a big wood. We was there for so many years, a lane-side, by the side of a wood. We were there for a long time, with the horses.

We travelled all over. We'd go to Skegness, we'd go to Yarmouth, all around London, spent the biggest half of my life in London. Me mother's people was there. We wouldn't get far away. Her mother lived until she was one hundred and ten, and she had two letters from the Queen. And they gave her two modern caravans, a little bit before she died. She was still in the horse van, but she still had the caravans - her old son used to live in one. She had one to put her bits of goods in. She was still in her old caravan, but she died in hospital, one hundred and ten years old. She had enough money on her, sewed on

underneath her clothes, to bury herself with. Me sister came to see her, and she said, *"Take that money and give it to my daughter, Ashy (my mother), and tell her to bury me with it"*, and the rest of the money that's left, she was to give it to her son Chasey. Some never had enough money to bury themself, they'd go around with a box to collect for a baby's funeral or something, in the old days, back when me mam was young.

Sometimes we'd travel a day and we'd pull out on a bit of a corner to give t'horses a break and to have a rest, and some times they'd move us on the same day. Yes, move us on about twice a day. The Police. Say you pulled on and there was a few houses anywhere in sight, they'd ring for the police. And when we was down a back lane sometimes we'd have a week, two weeks. In the laybyes, out in the wilderness, to be left alone. Anywhere close to a town or a village we couldn't have one day.

Move us on. That's all, they weren't bad. Just if you cheeked 'em. Many time my father would have the staff knocked on his head, for just trying to beg a day. We had to make a living. We never had no money. We'd only have enough money for one day's food. We'd have none the next. We had to get stopping somewhere to make a living.

When we were little we spoke the same language I'm talking now. Romany sometimes. Same as we're talking now, and Romany. I never learnt it, I just was born with it. It's like we're talking now - it's just our way, it was our life. I never know'd no other. Means that you can talk the one and the other. Me and Sakie can talk now, like foreign, like Indians, to one another. We never spoke no other way. My husband speaks what I speak, like we're the same. His mother and mine were first cousins, our fathers were first cousins. We're one relation.

I use to go out with me Granny, when I was about seven. She learnt me to sell pegs and tea strainers, combs, and little bits of things, needles and cottons and threads, you know. And then I used to say to me Mam, *"Let me come"*. She had me other sister with her. "No," she'd say, *"stay in and do a bit of work, and help to look after your handicapped brother and another little 'un"*. I kept saying, *"Let me come out to get some clothes for Christmas. Let me come, won't you Mam"*. So my Granny used to say to her, *"She's a good little hawker. Can take money, Shirley can. She can charm the flowers off the trees."* And so she took me out, and then I was given the wages, and she never let me stop home any more, she kept me out.

It's like work. Like the scrap men, sometimes they'll have a good day and sometimes hard. I liked it when I'd have a good day. But when it be hard, I'd get fed up. But they used to like me, the people in the houses, tell me I had nice teeth and nice eyes, and they'd buy 'cos I was nice looking. They'd buy to look at me. They'd ask me was me teeth real, and all things. These ain't me real teeth, you know. These is capped. But I had milk white, really lovely teeth. But I'm getting a bit older and lost them. I've got five caps in there. Well my teeth was like pearls, and everybody admired 'em. Some would buy just to talk to me. Most days I'd have a good tidy day.

I wouldn't cheek 'em. They'd send for the police, you daresn't cheek people around the houses. If you asked, *"Will you buy today, lady? Will you please have a look what I got"*, some will have a look and if they want anything they'll buy, but if you start pestering they'll send for the police. Say you're forcing your way in, forcing on 'em. Well I wouldn't. No. When they talked to me nice, well I'd talk to them, and then if I

Me mamus and me poor old sister Suzie jellin' down to the pani to durrek the foki and bickin' a few little bucki kuvers.

(Romanes)

OUT CALLING 1956 *Off to work in Skegness.*

had anything, they'd buy. *"Thank you, lady, God bless yer"*.

When I was a young girl I'd have a gramophone, with all the other girls, a wind-up gramophone, and get out and dance. I was the best dancer in them days amongst all the Travellers. Any kind of dance, the rumba or anything, the tango, rock and roll. Any dance that would come. I could put them off the floor. I won competitions. I was about 16 at Southend, there was a dance and before you'd go in there'd be a little holiday place, where you'd have a drink. I didn't drink but I'd have a Babycham. They'd give the time that the dance opened. And they'd be all putting the juke box on and start dancing rock and roll. They wanted to give me a job. I could have been famous. They used to give us all free drinks, and give us the best eat and drink for me to draw the custom, draw the people in.

My brother, he was famous for making flowers. Me brother, Tony Lee. He got a piece of elder, you go in the woods, and it grows, it's an elder tree, and he picks the smoothest pieces, and he saws them so long, and then they cut them in pieces like that with a saw, saws them in shape, and gets a peg knife, peels the top pieces off, and then the white you hold it on your knee, and start doing this, and it comes to a curly white chrysanthemum, and then we go and buy dye, you can have pink, yellow, red or any colour.

We'd have them three different colours, and you know the privets, we'd go to a garden and we'd knock at the door. *"Could we have some of them privets?"* Some ladies would say, *"No"*. We'd buy 'em, we'd have two shillings or whatever, and you'd break a piece off the top and there'd be a little hole in the top of the elder, made for the flower, and stick the privet on and maybe there'd be all green leaves, and looks like a fountain, and we used to sell them half-a-crown each.

There use to be the old ten shilling notes, and pound notes. Some would have eight, and some would have ten bobsworth, and they'd give us a red ten shilling note. Some would have two for five shillings, and if we had a hard day and we couldn't get rid of them, we'd let 'em go two shillings, or three for two shillings. We'd let 'em go cheap to get a bit of money, to make a living. And we'd do the pegs the same. Sell 'em half-a-crown a dozen, and then before we'd take 'em home, we'd let 'em go a bit cheaper to get a bit of money for food.

They'd do pegs the same way. A different stick. Different tree. Split 'em down the middle, and around the end to hold 'em, stop 'em from splitting, they'd have - you could buy pieces of tin from the tin factory, tip it narrow with the scissors, sharp scissors, and then put it around the bottom of the peg and knock a little nail in, to hold the peg. They ask us for the Gypsy pegs now, if you go anywhere, 'cos they were good pegs. And then they'd double-tin them to hold them tight, and to make them last. Well, they love the Gypsy pegs. Round the shops they'd order so many gross, and me Mother, not me, would take them to the shops and sell 'em.

I went to school once. I was about seven. I went with me shoes off. I used to play around - all the kiddies used to play around without their shoes. I can't remember what happened, but I came home crying, and I never went to school no more from this day to that. I can't remember what happened, but I know I went to school with my bare foot. I had shoes and I had the best of clothes, 'cos my Mother would have my clothes made in the dressmaker, but sometimes I would wear Wellingtons, but I just liked playing without shoes. I went to school whatever happened, I come home and I never did go to school again. One day schooling in my life. And I was about seven.

My brothers and sisters was like me. Never went to school. When the schoolman would come, we'd

hide. We wouldn't stay nowhere long enough. When the schoolman would come, we'd dodge him, and we'd go away the next day. Take off before he come back. My daughters went to school. Sakie didn't. Peter didn't. My gels did, but they didn't learn much, only little bits.

My own children, I did try to give them the chance. But they're clever. One gal passed the Test the first time - Shirley. They can tell prices of things, and they're fairly clever.

My grandchildren, they're all in school. Every one, barring the ones that ain't old enough. They've got to wait 'til they're five. But they're all in school. And half of 'em's all reading and writing. Good for 'em. If they want to get a bit of work, we don't trouble any more, down here we're trying to live, and all the daughters is on sites.

I was coming twenty-three when I got married, and still up to the day I got married, my Dad wouldn't let me get away. I had my sister bodyguarding me. She'd go home and tell my Mam everything. Very strict. I had to run away to have my husband.

Me Dad broke his heart over me. He cried for a long time over me. He loved me, he didn't want me to go. He talks about it now. He said it yesterday. He said to me, *"Shirley, you always wanted to get away and have a home of your own."* I said, *"Aye, Dad, when I got old enough. I want to have children."* He never did forgive me, no. He wanted me to stay home.

I got a sister at home, three years older than me. And I'd a mentally handicapped brother left at home. He died at fifty-nine. She stayed to look after him. Susie, she's still at home, looking after me Dad. I seen her yesterday. She's fit as anything. She could have got married, plenty of times, she had her chances, and the young men would go and ask me Dad for her, and then me Dad would run 'em off.

Susie could have had children, grandchildren, like I've got. When Susie got a little boy belonging to my younger sister. She copt leaving him with her and the child got attached. He calls me sister Mam. He's twelve year old, coming twelve on his birthday. He calls her Mam. She reared him, she reared him up. I used to look after these children. Never used to go nowhere, you know, no drinking. My husband drank a bit, and I'd stay in and wash these and put 'em to bed, and look after 'em, and wouldn't let nobody look after 'em, no baby-sitters. And I'd have a new baby and somebody would say, *"Can I look?"*, and I'd say, *"No"*. I'd let 'em look in there, but I wouldn't let 'em take my baby nowhere. When I'd go out in the day, my husband would look after 'em and then I'd have 'em the rest of the time and give him a break. Love my children, more than anything. That's only thing I've done good, you know, marriage and all me children.

Good boys, the boys were the better than the girls - there were two boys. I would have liked another boy, to be close to Sakie. Peter, we loves him but we don't see a lot of him. He moves around a bit. His wife likes it on the move. He got a big family - six. But Sakie was close to us. We always have him. When he was single, there'd be a funeral or a wedding or a party, but if anything was going on and I needed to get there, he'd get me there, no matter what, I'd get there with him. I had him to rely on. I've missed every hair on his head, but I'm thankful for his happiness, and wishes him every well, because he's happy and he's got a baby. All his life he wanted to get married and have a son, but he got a daughter, and I'd love her if she looked like Anna, I'd still love her. But we waited a long time for him to have a baby. His sisters is a little bit jealous, because I'm always talking about her, and I calls the other children Anna, and they get a bit jealous, but I love them all, but Anna's one of me favourites.

I was with my mamus-in-law and my husband's foki and I'm atchin' on Enfield Locks with my first tikna.

(Romanes)

ME AND SAKIE   *At Enfield Locks with my first baby.*

My girls I would rather for them to get married. I let 'em get married from me place. Go to the Office, buy 'em clothes, have a wedding breakfast and let 'em get married and get the worry off me mind. Frightened one of 'em would get killed coming back on journeys.

But Sakie's always been there; if you wanted a friend to sit with my daughter, he was there. He's paid us back more than enough. He loves his wife and he loves his baby. And if he had a son, I'd be very happy before I died. All his life he wanted a son, when he'd pass on, to leave the name of Lee to go on and on. But he got a lovely daughter and she's the model of him and he's very proud, and I'm very proud of her.

The young ones ain't doing nothing now. They tinker about. None of my people, not doing it any more. That's all finished. The children will get jobs and go to work, and live a normal life. Live a nice, clean, normal life, like other people, like other human beings. Have a nice job, nobody slamming the doors in 'em's face and ringing for the police.

You know it would be hard, don't you, with a door slammed in your face. Sometime calling you a "Gyppo". An' you didn't know no other life. That was it. The children they got no cause now. They can find themselves work, and come home and have em's tea and have a nice wash, dress up and go down the town. Come back at the right time. And lots of girls have cars and the boys got vans and cars and goes out and does a bit of work and do things. Different life and better.

I was more happier in the old days. I was young, wasn't I, and pretty. A pretty girl, and very slim, and could drive and do things, help me father and mother, clever girl. I could get a living, yes, telling fortunes. It's a thing, little bits of things you pick up, you know. But you're born - you can tell so much, so much you can't. It's a little gift. We only use it on the fairgrounds, when we travel with the fair in the summer, I loved it. We gave it up. Don't do no more. Don't go to work no more. Housewife now. Don't do nothing now.

Telling fortunes I give it up now, I'm Christian. It's wicked. Telling people things, you must leave it rest. We never knowed. We changed our religion. My husband hasn't. I have. We're Christian. We don't want none of that. We want to be kind. We want to help people, not frighten them, telling them things. We wants to help people. I try to help somebody, not frighten them and harm them.

Oh yes, I give my heart. But my husband won't let me go to the meetings very much, 'cos he's frightened. He's old fashioned. He's frightened I might change my way of life altogether completely. There's a lot of the women, they go all dolled up. I'm not the type. And they goes off. My husband don't want me to go. He loves me, he wants to keep me as I am. Jealous, a little bit jealous. He wants me for hisself, and to look after him.

I loves all me grandchildren, and I've devoted me life to me own family. All I want to do - live and see me family alright. Live day by day. When me time comes for me to go, I'm willing to go to God. But I only dread about my daughter. That's me only dread, when I go to leave my daughter behind. My handicapped, disabled daughter.

But I'm willing to go when me time comes. But we all would like to go sudden and quick. But all my life I've prayed for that, to go, I don't care how, but I wouldn't like to get killed, I would like to have a heart

attack, but wouldn't like a stroke, but I'd like to go quick, when the time comes. I'd like to go with a heart attack, and I wouldn't like to live too old. I wouldn't like to become a nuisance, like me dear old Dad nearly is. You know, seventy will do me - seventy-odd. See a bit more of Janet.

It's a different life. It's changed our life completely. We're just living the same as you now, nearly. We haven't travelled for eight years. I do go to Appleby, to have a holiday, a week's holiday, and then we're back. I was on a site for three years and a half at Sheffield, three year and a half at Wakefield, I've been here nine months. That's in eight years.

If I was young, I'd be on the road now. If I was young, I'd be still on the move and around. Now, I'm getting old. Me husband's sixty-four in May. Seven years older than me. We're getting too old for the roads. A lot of the young people have the summers run, then they comes and parks and settles down for the winter. I haven't been on the road for eight years. Don't go nowhere. That's why we tried to get this bit of land to settle. We don't want to go on the roads. We bought this bit of land and we'll leave it to Sakie - he's the main one - he's oldest. Leave for him to do what he likes. He'll have his sister. It's up to him, left to him, he's my oldest child.

There's a lot of old people gone in Council houses, glad to get out. Don't ask me why, I don't know. Can't live the life. We'll sleep in our old caravan. My old mother died in her caravan. I don't want to go into a house. I'm happy in whatever sort of caravan it is. A lot of noise goes on on the site. We're peaceful here. Nobody bothers us. It's nice and quiet. That's all we wants to do - live and be quiet and have peace. I'd travel in the summer, you know, and settle in the winter, if I was young. I wouldn't travel forever.

Well, we're trying ain't we? We've had a try. When we were on the roads travelling, they'd say, *"Go on a site."* When we'd go on a site - all ructions. And then we do this, and now they're trying to get us out. Well, what can we do? Go in a house and die unhappy. Be broken hearted - like the Indians. Like putting the Indians in houses - you might as well be dead.

We want to live here 'til our time comes. And we're quiet and we ain't doing anything, we're just living.

I don't go out, I only goes to June, my own little daughter, my youngest daughter, next door. Shirley, with the children, comes down here and visits me. There's a bus, there, going on that road, going on the way to Leeds and I can go shopping wherever I want, on the bus. And there's little shops around me where I can walk to.

Jimmy Berry - wagon painter

YORKSHIRE LIFE ILLUSTRATED
OCTOBER 1962 NUMBER 10 VOLUME XVI

'The caravan, at York Castle Museum, was built in 1897 and is a perfect example of the type known as a "Leeds Wagon".

When the museum acquired it, it needed painting, and only a Gypsy could do that properly.

The museum staff visited Topcliffe Gypsy fair, chatted with Romanies and finally traced Jimmy Berry, one of the only two practitioners of the caravan painter's art in this country.

This picture was taken when Jimmy had almost completed his colourful task, which lasted about two months.'

Sara Ann Morrison

I was born on Boxing Day 1929, in County Waterford, Ireland. I wouldn't change my life because I like my life. I like the way I was brought up - honest. I was brought up to be honest by my Mam and Dad and not to be vulgar with people. Be kind to people and they'll be kind to you.

...tells her story

Yes, that's what my Mother and Father taught us. Be kind to people and be nice to people and they'll be nice to you. I've always done that, always tried, and it's always worked. My parents were Gypsies. I don't mind being called a Gypsy, it doesn't worry me. Well, it doesn't make no difference, does it? You can say Traveller or Gypsy - it doesn't make no difference. You see, my father was English. He was born in Leeds, somewhere here. I don't know where. My grandmother came from this country, but where I don't know. And my mother's father and mother, well one was from Kent - London - but I don't know where - where they were born or 'owt like that. 'Cos a lot of my people I don't know, love, never met them. My father ended up going to Ireland when he was young. I don't know why they went over. They went travelling - went to Ireland.

I was born there, in Ireland. I'm the oldest. I have two sisters and three brothers. We were just born in a place and we went on. We never settled. You know what I mean: only a few days, a week or a fortnight. I was born in a Gypsy wagon. We had a nurse and a doctor, from the town or village or wherever it was. They come down in case the mother needed them. Well, a nurse or a doctor would be there anyway, wouldn't she? A midwife. There's a lot of people think that, because you're a Gypsy, you're just born. It's not like that, love. No, you have to have a nurse - a midwife - course you have, love, they're not that stupid. You'd get into serious trouble, wouldn't you?

Mine were born in hospital. I was safer, I thought, in hospital. I always liked to go to hospital with my children, to have them. I've got three girls, no four girls and five boys. And grandchildren - oh, love - I've lost count of them; couldn't tell you how many I've got. They've all got good families, like six and five and all of this.

My children was christened in churches. It was very important to me because I'm a Protestant. I believe in God. My mother and father believed in being christened; every one of us. I don't think that it is not right if you're not christened or baptised, do you? You don't need to rent a Church to believe in the Lord. You can pray wherever you're at, if you need God.

My mother used to sell flowers and that: pegs and carpets and all sorts. Mam sometimes used to make them, and sometimes used to buy them in old sales. But not the flowers; they made them themselves. My brother used to make wooden flowers. That's all a thing of the past. We don't do it now - died out. I started selling with my Mam when I was about fifteen or sixteen, I should think. Teenagers sell flowers and pegs and that. We only went out round the doors. We selled, and if we didn't, it never bothered us. You always lived - you never went hungry.

Dad was a horse dealer. Buy horses and sell them at the Fairs. They're famous in Ireland - they still are. All the dealers are there now, you know; still selling horses and buying them. Caravans and donkeys - everything - you mention it and they buy it and sell it. He used to go to the Fairs and sell them and buy them. That's all I knew about because, them days, they didn't let the children know the business. You know what I mean? That was a secret sort of side.

The girls followed the mother and the boys followed the father.

Me Mam and Dad atchin' on the drom side. Me Mam's got the jukel and behind them is the varda.

(Romanes)

My Dad was a horse dealer and my Mum used to sell flowers, pegs, combs and whatever she could get. Mum is holding the dog in front of our wagon.

We travelled all of Ireland, north and south, the thirty-six counties. We just stopped maybe a month in one place for the winter, if we could stay in it, but we never bothered, like - over Christmas and over the holidays, and then we moved on. So we never got involved with nobody. Now do you know what I mean? With local people, that's what I mean.

We had a horse caravan. Horse wagons in those days. The old bow topped ones. They were nice. Lovely to live in. Different to living in a modern caravan. They were smaller, plus they were easy to handle. Just put your horse on and then you could go on. That's the way they looked at it, I think. Just hitched your wagon to your team and on you went, like the cowboys. And all they needed to call us was Indians, and we were right.

Me and me sisters havin' us pictures taken in a proper studio near Glasgow in Scotland.

This is me and my two sisters, Betty and Ada. It was taken in Kirkintilloch outside Glasgow in 1947. We weren't long over from Ireland.

Well, when we left Ireland to come to this country, we sort of got into the motors and trailers. I think I was about eighteen or nineteen years of age, or something like that, when I came across to England. We went to Scotland first. That's where I got married. He was a Gypsy as well, but all his people settled; they all had houses - didn't travel as much as we did. But they were still Travellers. They used to deal in horses; get scrap and things like that. Different things.

When we got married, we stayed together for a bit with my own family, and then we went on about our business. You do do that; you stay with your family for a bit and then you go on. When you leave your family, love, you're leaving your life, ain't yer, really? Part of your life, ain't yer?

But we always met up, you know. We only go away for a while and then come back. Well, we'd always know where one another was - places they stayed - and we'd go down.

I'm atchin here at this kushti place - me and all my chavies. My mush is out dickin' for his livin'. The kakavi is boiling on the yog and the chavies were playing, waiting for their hobin.

(Romanes)

My sister has just come home from hawking. The food is on the fire cooking, waiting for my husband to come home from work. The children are playing and waiting for their meal.

We were on the road. He used to travel up and down, you see. Didn't settle in a house, because he didn't like a house. Some likes to stay put and some likes to go on. His family settled because they liked it.

To start off, back then, I had a horse wagon, and then we got rid of them and got the motor and trailer. It was quicker to get about - we thought, anyway. Although I handled horses all my life; well, I used to ride them and drive them and yoke them myself. I used to be able to put harness on and drive. It didn't bother me. I wasn't frightened of them because I was raised with them, you see. On the motorways it's dangerous now; you couldn't do it, not with the horses, no.

I wouldn't go on the road with horses now, love, it's too dangerous. And I wouldn't advise me children, because you've got some chance in a motor, haven't you, yes, but you haven't on a horse.

This is me, my husband, Jackie, my daughter, Nora and me grandson, little Tony.

I went with my husband to Appleby Fair. Then I used to go for the day, but not to stay on it, you know. When you've got little children it's dangerous, very dangerous. That's what used to keep me back.

Didn't mind going for the day, because you've got to be careful, haven't you, to keep an eye on the kids, 'cos there's loads and loads of horses. They trot them up and down, and then they have horse racing and all sorts. It's nice.

Now, you could learn more from one day going to it than you could staying here for a week, because a couple of hours watching the horses and watching the people - very interesting. Oh, there's loads of people there.

❋

They all come from all over to go to Appleby, because they come to get their fortune told, they get the hand-reading there, don't they? Well I can read your hand, or I can read fortunes. If anybody asks me I

do it. I give it up, I don't bother now. Nobody taught me; it's in you. You can either do it or not. I done the crystal and the hands.

Oh yes, it's the real thing. You can get a Gypsy with a crystal to do the right thing for you, and read your fortune the proper way, but well, there's a lot pretend, isn't there? That's the money business, isn't it?

I never would hurt anybody's feelings. To upset them for the day - how could you do that? You couldn't, could you? It wouldn't be in you, love. You can have a smile with it and a laugh, get some fun with it, can't you? It depends the way you look at it.

You can get your fortune told at Appleby Fair like in the picture.

This is outside the 'Eccles' in 1982 when we were stopping in Cross Green, Leeds. I'm with Nora, Roy and baby Nora.

I give up working a few years back. I used to sell flowers and that. All kinds of flowers. Anywhere - villages, towns or anything. But we don't do it now. Now you get Income Benefit, now, don't you? That's the best way, because you're sure of your money and you're sure of your food.

At my age it was hard enough, love, sometimes. Fancy me walking down that road, bunch of flowers in my hand. I'll tell you something, love, it's not safe. You can't go around having bags in your hand, because people think you've got loads of money and you get mugged and robbed and all sorts.

Watching the horses and meetin' people at Appleby Fair. Travellers have been coming here for hundreds of years.

In 1983 we were stopping in Cross Green between the factories. My two daughters, Yvonne and Nora with my grandchildren Robert and Lisa.

The Gypsy life has changed now. I would like to go back on the road. I loved it on the road, love. Well you see different places and different people. It's intelligent. But there's no places to go, is there? It's not the same. It's changed, because you can't stay on the side of the roads now. You get put on. You know what I mean? You've got to go. Well, the Council or the Police or whatever moves you on.

We never got into arguments, well not really, not in Leeds, because I stayed for three and a half years at one place. And then I was nearly four years in a place I come off when I came here. And we were all around Leeds for years. You know, up and down, bits of ground and places. No, I wasn't really bothered. I never had much trouble with the Police, 'cos we kept ourselves to ourselves. You know what I mean. As I do now. I keep myself to myself. I don't get mixed up in other people's troubles. I still carry on in my own way, and I prefer it that way.

Well I would love to travel if I could. But all my family are here, and they're all settled here, so then there's no point in me going anywhere, is there? Only for a holiday, if I can. When you're settled you meet friends, don't you? When we come here to Leeds we met all our friends, my family did, and very nice friends when we come to Leeds. We've been around Leeds now for over thirty years.

I'm only here since Christmas - week before Christmas I came here. Never was on a site. Only once in Newcastle. I've never been on a place where there's hot and cold water - put it that way. So that makes a difference.

We were stopping here for years. It was a great place to stop amongst the factories in Cross Green. We knew everyone around here and no-one bothered us. This was back in 1985.

You know, I never had any chance to go to school, so I can't read nor write. But nobody can do me out of money; I can count money.

Well, I've got a daughter-in-law can read, and I've got grandchildren can read, write me letters or read me letters. If I didn't have them, I'd have to go to somebody else who I could depend on. Because I'm not ashamed, you see.

The only thing I regretted, if I went in to sign for my money in my pension book, if my daughter's not there, I've got to put a cross.

But now at my Post Office - well I call it 'my' Post Office, it's not 'my' Post Office, but I've been getting my money there for years - and my daughter can draw my money and sign for it. Because I'd have to put a cross.

But he doesn't bother about that, and I know that. They don't bother about these things, you know, because it's your signature, and that's no bother.

But it would be nice if I could sign my name.

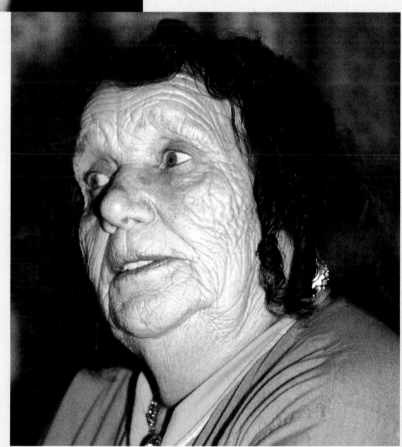

Sara Ann's Brother

ROY GENTLE AT APPLEBY IN 1970

We always lived in wagons and I've still got that wagon.

We were horse dealers and we used to have it written on the side of the wagon -

R. GENTLE, HORSE DEALER, LONDONDERRY.

Jack Hope painted the wagon up for us. He drew out the patterns and then painted it and put on the original scrawls.

The dog is Spring, an Irish Wolfhound. He was good for killing hares and rabbits, getting me dinner, whatever jumped up he got.

We had Spring for fifteen years.

He was a good dog, number one.

At Appleby we used to have the one place to stop, by a big tree so we could tie the stallion and be near the trough.

There was nine brothers of me Dad and all the cousins.

It was all wagons those days. Before that we were on the roadside, they were all packed in and the wagons went on for two miles right down to the river.

You enjoyed yourself walking one to the other. We used to have fun at the fire singing old songs and someone would have a melodeon and guitars going and there was some good songs sung at Appleby.

They used to do a bit of dancing in the road.

We did it our way and that was it.

158

Roy Gentle - horse dealer

Ada North

Well, my name's Alma Ada Kindon, better known as Kendal. I was born in West Hartlepool on the 29th March 1928. I come from a family of eleven.

...telling about her life

I was the youngest girl. I had three brothers, well me Mam had sets of twins so you know, I'm not going to go right into details. We lived in wagons; we had accommodations and carts. Me Mam used to go out hawking and get us a bit of bread every day, we used to wait for her bringing us a sweet home. If all the begged clothes and the begged bread was out of me, there'd be very little left of me today. I appreciate the way I was brought up; we were always taught to respect people, keep ourselves to ourselves, we weren't allowed to run wild, or go round other people's places when they weren't at home.

Me Dad used to get up on a morning, find a bit of stick to light a fire, and whoever was stopping with us he'd fill their kettle and put it around our fire on the kettle prop. Me Mam would get out of bed and wash herself, 'cos we were very clean people, we always believed in washing before we touched the clean pots and things. She'd fry a bit of bacon, an egg, whatever was on the go. And she'd get us washed, we'd have our breakfast, we'd play around, she'd go out hawking, me Dad perhaps take her on a cart if it was a few villages nearby where we were staying - they'd go and hawk the villages. Me Dad would hawk brooms off a cart to the farmers, me Mam would beg a few taties, or carrots or a turnip, a few eggs, a nice old boiling chicken for the pot. When she come home of a night time, she'd feed us and we'd look in on what she'd begged that day, and then she'd do a bit o' washing, hang it on the hedge hoping for morning that it would be dry.

Then Appleby Fair would be comin' nigh on, we'd start getting ready. She'd buy a bit of print, have us frocks made for me and me sisters, bits of things for the boys. We'd come up the road and we'd pull in Stoney Lane, have a week there, while me Mam went hawked all the little bits of villages, and then we'd pull on Thirsk. In Thirsk we'd get ourselves all prettied up, the wagons cleaned up and tidied up, the horses brushed, the harness cleaned, packed up and then we'd go the next four mile to Appleby. The longest four mile I've ever seen in me life! And then we'd go in the field at that time maybe have to be paying five shilling a week, five shilling for to go in the field, and the men would start trading - horses, carts or whatever - at that time fifty bob a horse - there was no big moneyed horses at them times. And everybody shared what they had. The children would play around, the younger end of the people of a night would walk onto the bridge, they'd have a bit of music, have a dance, the older people would have a sing-song round the fire. It was really a lovely time.

You knew exactly where everybody stayed, right up to the White House. Me, in my teens, dying to go to a dance, daren't mention it. No girl went to the dances - not many, anyway. But I used to sneak off, couldn't sleep at night because I used to talk in my sleep and they'd know I'd been to a dance and I'd get killed. And we used to have a bit of fun on the roads and put the headlights on, them that had cars which were very lucky. I'm talking now in the war time, when petrol was on ration and you could go a long way with £1.50, thirty shilling, you were a millionaire - especially a young woman. And we'd flaunt ourselves and walk up and down, fancying ourselves like young girls do.

I've gone to Appleby Fair since I was a baby in arm, a little girl, a young woman, a married woman and a granny, now I'm a great-granny, God help us. But things have changed a lot now. They just go where they want, they get in a motor, go here and go there, go to the dances, but what harm is there in it now, as long as they don't do anything wrong?

And that's all I can tell people. Think about and respect your parents, 'cos they're the best friend you've got, you know.

Around the yog there's a kakavi cosh and a mutter mangri kurra.

(Romanes)

It's 1944 and we are camping at Stokesley Batts waiting to go to Topley Fair. I am second on the left, aged sixteen.

And then they have funerals, and they have big funerals. When anybody dies belonging to them, they wake 'em for three or four days, they have enormous funerals, and they have big christenings, and when a child is born it's loved from the minute it comes into the world, but the woman is never allowed to touch anything of the cups.

Me sisters, when they had children, me Mam looked to them. They had their own plate, saucer, cup, a knife and a spoon, and when they were churched and the child was christened, they were thrown out. They weren't allowed to touch food 'til they'd been in a House of God. That's our belief.

We're very funny on our views and things, we have a dish to wash the cups up, and we have a dish for the vegetables, and one to bake in. We don't believe in sitting with our bare feet because it's not done in Gypsy life. We'd share anything we had, but we're a very close community and we're from the Tenth century. Do believe it, it can be proved!

Story Twelve

We don't like to get married out; a lot of us are - including meself - but I'm not going to say it doesn't work, sometimes it does, it just depends who you get. I've got some grandchildren; they've married their own kind of people, and me daughter married into her own class of people - very happy and contented at the present moment - might have a black eye tomorrow. There's not really a lot I can say, but I enjoyed me life, I'd a good upbringing, strict; I appreciate how I was brought up, I brought my children up the same. If we can do any good for anybody we do it, and if you do any good for anybody, keep it to yourself. Them you do good for shouldn't forget it, and you shouldn't talk about it. That's how we've been raised.

This is my cousin Ada's wedding to Dennie Evans. You can see all the Crown Derby. The wedding cake was made by Sentabel Evans. This was a family celebration in 1949.

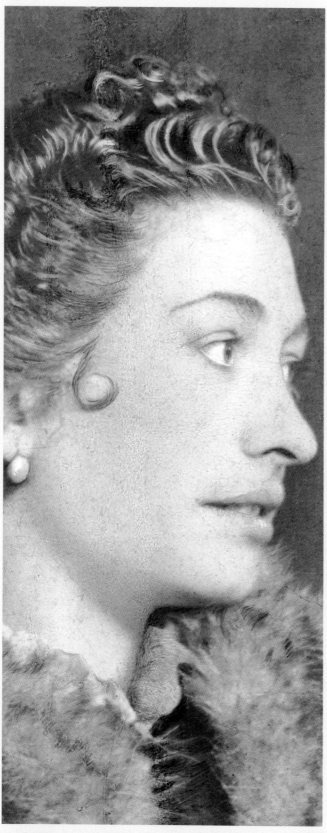

In 1953 I was 25, still single, and enjoying my stay at Doncaster Races with my pal, Dixie Boswell.

Now for schooling - I've been to school. I went to school in Stockton-on-Tees - a school called St Anne's. I couldn't read and write - I couldn't do anything really. But the reason why you went to school - the war started in 1939. It was on a Sunday - I'll never forget it. We were all ready to go to Doncaster Races. My elder brother, Kazy, he was on the races, but the war started. Me Mam thought we were going to get bombed the next minute. So we didn't go. We were put into school. I liked it. The children didn't care for us because we were Gypsies. We had a big Bill Wright's wagon, we had a tent. I liked school a lot; they learnt me a few things. They learnt me how to knit and how to crochet. The teachers wasn't bad; there was one especially - a Miss Greenwood - she was a very nice woman. I'll always remember. And I used to go to the School races, egg and spoon race, and things like that. But I still didn't learn to read 'til I was fourteen, and I just learnt meself, picking a book up.

And if we went to Yarm, we'd maybe be in Yarm for a fortnight, in Yarm back lane, and me Mam would have us in school then. She used to say *"I know where you are while I'm looking for bread."* So we went to school then.

Me brothers went to school, but we don't believe in girls learning the things that they learn today. They'll know enough, learn enough for themselves. And I don't think it's really necessary for a girl to have a good education, 'cos they get married, they have kids, and they don't go to work, they go out hawking, looking for their living like they've been taught.

The boys go - I mean a schoolmaster can't learn a lad to judge a ton of scrap, or anything like that. That's a thing that comes to 'em. It's like our Billy Lee's family. They can all read and write. They learnt while the war was on, when they were working on the camps, doing a bit of duty for their King and country. And my brothers was in the army - both of 'em. Me Dad was in the 1914 war; he was in Flanders, and Dusseldorf in Germany. So we did fight for our country and we are English but we don't get treat very well.

We've been shifted at 3 o'clock in the morning - rain, snow, blow. We've been treat like dogs. I was on the field near the site and I had the bunks out, and they just fetched a bulldozer and bulldozed everything in, and they were just going to rip the trailer onto a Council wagon. If it hadn't been for Jimmy Lowther, he came down and got me off, because me husband was out looking for his living and I'd had the day in to wash and clean.

And then there was another good schoolteacher, a Mrs Syrett. An angel, she was. They come to shift my daughter, she'd been on the life machine in the Infirmary, having her first baby, she was very bad with her nerves, she was in the Intensive Care, and they said that she would die. Thank God, the doctors did save her, but she was in a terrible way for months and months, and she was on the side of me on a plot. They came with two Black Marias, dogs and a load of policemen. Her husband wasn't in - he was out looking for his living - she couldn't handle a baby because she'd got a third degree burn in hospital, she had a fall out of bed and they didn't tell us about it, and she was in a coma for 175 hours. And what had happened was they wouldn't allow you to double up on the site - you could maybe stay a month doubled up, and they just come and shift you. Mrs Syrett said, *"Well I think it's a disgrace. A woman with a baby a fortnight old - coming to tow her trailer off."*

And they just pulled it off and twisted it round, but they didn't get the chance because one of the lads that was on the ground said, *"Wait a minute, I'll pull it down."* And he pulled it down on the lane as you come up to the site. There was only one site there at the time. And he pulled it in the lane till her husband come home, then they had to move. And she was really, really ill. We've been tormented and tortured.

I put washing out there one day, and it wasn't Ring's it was some other name (it's Ring's I believe, the factory, now) and I'd put all me washing out and the boss from the place come and cut the line and danced on it. *"Get away, you dirty Gypsy."* And God forgive me he was a Jew and he should have remembered what Hitler did to him - to his people - he should have thought: Well my people suffered and I'm doing the same to these people.

And we have been made to go off and I've begged and the people's come to move us on and I've said, *"Look, you go home to your house tonight. Where do we go?"* 'Cos there was nowhere to go - there was no room on the site. And the man has been kind enough and let us stay till Monday, but we've kept our promise and we've moved on - we've had the weekend on the mint fields and things like that - but it's not done today.

There's no place at all you can stay in Leeds, and there should be, there should be a transit site for people that just come in for a couple of weeks and go off, because the people on Leeds site won't move 'cos if they do, where can they go? There's nowhere for 'em to go in Leeds.

The children's been born here, the children's married in Leeds, it's their home. There should be one place built in Leeds - a field of any kind - that there's a toilet put on and a skip - and if the people that come on it don't keep it clean, well the next time the people will know what to do - keep 'em going.

It's their own fault if they don't keep their places clean. It's up to them, isn't it, to keep the places clean, but there should be a transit site, for just people that's coming in and out of it.

When I first came to Leeds it was quite nice. We used to go to the pictures. We used to stay on the Lemmy. We used to stay on Brown Lane. There's a school there now. There's Matthew Murray's on there now. We used to stay on there, go for little shops.

My Dad had donkeys and ponies; he used to do the Gala at Temple Newsam and the park.

The lads used to go out looking for their living around Leeds, which wasn't too bad to get a bit of bread. We weren't millionaires, I don't think we ever will be. As I said before, everybody knew where they were coming to. And the shop people were nice to us. We used to go take the washing to the wash house. But all that's gone now. There's no place in Holbeck, Hunslet or anywhere you can stay. Those that have bought their own places. They still get hounded. Can't get them passed so what's the good of buying them. Well there's nothing else I can tell yer, only just think about us for a change - We're not all bad.

I'm settled down now. I'm in a house. I don't like it, but there again, nowhere else I can go, 'cos I can't drive so I wouldn't want to be on a site, so I'm in a little house - one up and one down - by meself, and I'm contented.

I did come in a house. I thought, well, I'll go in a house. But then, I was only in it twelve months and me husband died ... you blame yourself. And me boy wasn't the same when I come in a house, 'cos he mixed with the wrong company. When he was up on the site, he mixed with his own class. He come down here, got in the pubs, and mixed with this, that and the other.

This is in 1985. We are trying to get stopping on this ground in Holbeck and stop the eviction of Traveller families already pulled onto the ground. You can see some of the demonstrators with their posters. Many of 'em weren't Travellers themselves but felt strongly enough to turn up and help.

I'm with Adam and Robert.

He was never the same lad after that. And that's the truth. But as I say, you can't blame houses, you can't blame the town, but you can blame the company he gets with.

❋

I'd rather live in a caravan. I would, tomorrow, definitely. Because you're pinned in - you're in gaol - we've never been used. We're like birds - we like to fly. It's a terrible thing. I sit in here night and day. I do, honestly. It's a terrible life. I mean, I've got a sister on a site, she's seventy. I've got a brother - he's on his own, he's seventy-five and he wouldn't come into a house for nobody. He's got his own little trailer, he keeps it clean, he cooks for himself. Same as me sister, down there, she won't come off, she wouldn't come in a house. The Travelling life has gone. It's gone. It's only these now that go to Appleby that try to keep it up. There'll always be Appleby, and there'll always be Lee Gap.

❋

Jack with our John and my niece, Ada Gaskin, at Lee Gap Fair, 1974.

On camp at Smallways, 1961. A traditional stoppin' place for Travellers, on our way to Appleby Fair.

Oh, well I want the young ones to know where their roots are. I've got some little nieces and nephews at York - me brother Jim's children - and I took the little girl to Appleby on the train, and I said to her on the train, *"Natalie, do you know what Romanes is?"* She said, *"I know a little bit, Aunt Ada, but not a lot."* So I said, *"Well, I'll learn you it, but that's some'at we've got to keep to ourselves, that's our only defence when we're talking among ourselves. So, we'll have to learn you, and you must never forget it, and when you get married you've got to learn your children it."* And I hope my children keep up the life, and my grandchildren. Well, I know one will. That red-headed one we've got, Joe's lad, I know he loves Appleby, and his Mam says, *"I wish he was married so I don't have to come meself."* He'll always go, I know he will.

And God forgive me for saying this - I'm in Leeds and I'll die in Leeds. I'll be buried in Cottingley Hall, 'cos there's more Gypsies in Cottingley Hall than there's house-dwellers, now. And if I was near there my one wish would be to take me all around Appleby - round the hill in a coffin, in a hearse and then bring me back to Leeds but it'd take for ever, so I don't think I'll manage that bit.

This is me on Appleby Fair in the 1960's with our John and all my friends and relations. It was a great time.

Travellers is famous for havin' lots of colourful pottery and most of all for havin' Crown Derby. There's tea services and pottery figures all made in Crown Derby. But years ago, in my Mam's days, they didn't have Crown Derby - they were lucky if they had a pretty cup to drink out of, but today it's a thing that these younger ones want - even meself including.

I think you just like it 'cos it's colourful, and it's something there, if you've got your money down. You can always get money 'forit or onit', but it's a silly thing 'cos it can break. But it's something nice to pass on to your children in't it.

I'll pass it on to my girls. I've got some for me boy, I've got some for me grandchildren. I gave me grandaughter when she got married, and I've some for me other grandchildren.

I've got five left to go, and I've got a little bit o' some'at for 'em all.

At a wedding with friends Lilly Moor and Nellie Lowther. We've had some good times together.

CAMPS IN LEEDS

This is Aunt May and Miley's children, Jacqueline and Eileen Connors, with their niece, Mary Purple. They are playing on their camp in Armley, Leeds when they were only small. In the background you can can see the family trailers and also the piles of bricks and rubble that the council used to try to block off these camps and stop us using them.   Kathleen Doran

This is Aunt Chicken and Joe's children, Paddy, Jimmy, Cuckoo and Eileen with Ruby Kelby and Mary Doran.

There is a heap of old scrap iron behind them and the boys are making up some bikes to play with. They are taking turns on the bikes 'cos there'd only be two bikes between twenty childer.

Kathleen Doran

As the council were knocking down the houses, the Traveller families were pulling on the waste ground for somewhere to stop. There was only one caravan site at Cottingley Springs for fifteen families and the rest were left on the roadside to find somewhere themselves.   Bill Doran

ARMLEY 1978

1970's

This is Jacqueline, my cousin, she is letting on to be a 'Mammy', making tea for her cousins, Cuckoo and Eileen Moloney and Jerry Mike's children.

Kathleen Doran

This is Jerry Mike's children, Elizabeth and May May, playing in their 'Dolly House' they'd made from bricks and stuff from round the camp.

Kathleen Doran

This camp is in the old streets off Tong Road, in Armley, Leeds in 1978. These types of camps were rough and ready, but at least they were somewhere to pull for a few weeks or a few days. The council and police used to come and move you off. The families didn't get much chance to put the children to school as they didn't get stopping long enough.

Bill Doran

ARMLEY 1978

CAMPS IN LEEDS

The childer are making 'Dolly Houses' with bricks, crates and old furniture from round the camp. There's Jacqueline and Eileen Connors, Eileen Moloney, all my cousins with Lyddie and Ruby Kelby and Jerry Mike's children.   Kathleen Doran

The children were more friendly then, and played well together. The people were a lot better to each other. Times were hard, but there was a better atmosphere amongst Traveller families. People used to share and help each other out.   Janie Doran

ARMLEY 1978

1980's

This camp was behind the University, off Blackman's Lane. We used to stop around there for years. That's Lawrence Ward's family stopping with my sister's family, May and Miley Connors in 1983. It was a good camp in the summer, like a big field for the children to play in.

Bill Doran

This is Aunt May's trailer, a small 'Portmaster', with all the chrome jackcans with the bath in the middle and the dustbin and the coal scuttle for the fire.

Kathleen Doran

BLACKMAN'S LANE 1983

CAMPS IN LEEDS

This was down 'The Dip', Rothwell as you go for Rothwell auction. We stopped on there for years. Old Jim Varey was on there first and he was last off. It was a bad camp in the winter 'cos you couldn't get on or off with the ice on the slope. There was no water, electricity or toilets, but at least we got stopping. It's all done away with now.

Joey Lowther

ROTHWELL 1984

1980's

This is behind St. James's Hospital. The caravans were pulled on the school playing fields. It was a nice place to stay in the summer with the grass for the children to play on and somewhere for the ponies to graze. The families were moved off after a few weeks.

Bill Doran

PRIMROSE HILL 1985

175

CAMPS IN LEEDS

This was an old coalyard in Armley, Leeds. We were on and off there for almost a year. It was a good camp as you were in the middle of Armley and the shops and baths were handy. The bad thing about the camp was the black mud from the coal dust that ruined all the carpets in the trailers and you couldn't keep it out. We were all on there, Dorans, Connors, Moloneys, Kelbies and Prices. It's all built on now and the camp has been done away with.
Bill Doran

ARMLEY 1985

This was 'The Brick Camp' and we was on there for years. It was handy for everything, just at the back of the bank in Holbeck. We pulled on top of the bricks when they pulled the factory down. We got shifted off in the end and it got done away with. There's new factories on there now. Fourteen years ago, in 1984, our Shirley's Tiny was born on here.

Mary Lowther

HOLBECK 1986

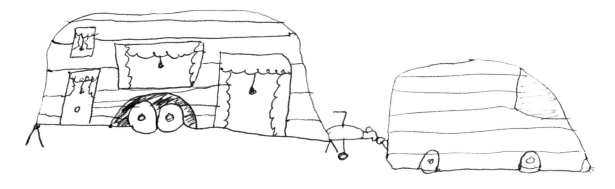

177

This was the old Railway Yard in Hunslet opposite Tetleys Brewery. There are all the children with Tom, the Traveller teacher, waiting to go in Peter the Schoolman's School Van that used to go around all the camps at that time. There are the children from all these families Tommy and Rose Cawley, Maggie Mc Donagh, Mick and Kay Connors, Aigie and Jim Doyle, Jessie and Chuckens, Ivor Lee, the Welsh families and our Janie.   Bill Doran

This is Philomena Doyle, Kay Connors and Mary Purcell on 'The Railway Yard Camp' in Hunslet, Leeds in 1983. The trailers in the background belong to the Welsh Gypsies, the Lees, who were stopping on this camp with us.   Bill Doran

HUNSLET 1983

1980's

This was 'Miggey Woods', Middleton, 1987. A good camp. You was on top of everything. It was a clean, open camp with plenty of space. And you got stopping, this was a camp for years. It's all finished now. They've built a sports centre on it.

Joey Lowther

This is the Sheridans, the furniture men, camping up the York Road in Leeds, near Killingbeck Hospital, back in the eighties. They travel all over the country and there are always thirty or forty trailers together. It's like one big family, the Sheridans, Gammels and Quilligans.

Bill Doran

MIDDLETON & KILLINGBECK 1987

CAMPS IN LEEDS

Woodhouse Moor was a nice clean camp, good for the children. Across the road was a big green field and a park for the children to play on. We'd cross them over the road to play on the park. We were stoppin' on there in 1989, waiting for the new site at Cottingley to be done. We got a few weeks before being moved on. You were near everything, the shops and the garage. Everyone got on and it was a good camp.

Diane Smith

WOODHOUSE MOOR 1989

1980's

We were up in a big field in Cross Green, 1989. Mary, Kathleen, Eileen, Sarah, Bridget and the famous Danny and their cousins Margaret and Tom Hanrahan. They were good old days when the children were younger and could just play about together in lovely green fields.

Maidie Connors

CROSS GREEN 1989

Leeds Eviction - 1985

The shades are stoppin' every lork coming onto the mollie or goin' off.
(Cant)

HALTON MOOR - AN 'UNOFFICIAL' CAMP - 1985

The police are stopping any vehicles from coming onto or going out of this unofficial camp. We could not get water, go shopping, collect the children or get off working.

We were all shifted by the police the next day. They escorted us out of Leeds making sure that we were not stopping anywhere by blocking all the roads with police cars.

We were forced out towards the main A1 road in a long convoy. It was the day of the big winds when all the radio broadcasts were telling people not to travel because of the dangerous high winds, especially in high-sided vehicles!

We refused to go on and stopped at the entrance to Micklefield Coalyards. We still had the children at school back in Leeds. When the police went away we got on the camp.

The teachers managed to collect all the children and find the new camp, but it took hours!

Halton Moor Camp

We couldn't go to the gripas or collect the gaulyers from school.
(Cant)

The convoy of evicted families and their trailers got stoppin' on Micklefield Coalyards. There was plenty of space, but we kept close together in case of any trouble.

Angelina Smith

I was born in Layfields Yard, Darlington, County Durham on the 19th March 1954. They were 'yards' then, they weren't 'sites'. You used to pay so much a week. It wouldn't be much, it'd be probably two bob a week then, to stay in the Yard all week, well, all the year.

...sharing memories in words

I've been in Leeds about thirty-seven years now, altogether. I've been married to my husband, Michael, now for twenty-six years and have three children. My children are Michael junior, eleven and two married daughters, Tracey and Joanne. I have three grandsons with a new grandchild expected in September - hopefully a granddaughter this time. My grandchildren are the fifth generation, so that is five lots of changes. Their life has got easier in living conditions but harder in other ways. Me Dad was born in a Yard in Hartlepool, and me Dad would have been seventy-three gone January. It were me Dad that decided to come to Leeds.

We lived in Darlington all them years, and then all of a sudden he just got a brainwave, he said, *"We've been in this little town too long, it's time we left it."* Just out of the blue, and we were really settled there, but it's what he wanted to do, and then we came to Leeds, but when we came to Leeds there was no such thing as sites then, so the first place we stopped in Leeds was up on the Trees, in Middleton. And then from there we went onto the Dog Track, and then it was nearly always round Hunslet, and in the summertime we used to go up to Norfolk, picking the fruit, but we always come back to Leeds for the winter.

When we came to the Trees in Middleton, it was like a big green field and there were scattered trees up and down it. When we first went on there, there was nobody on, only us. It was late at night when we'd come from Darlington to Leeds. And we pulled on that. Me Dad said, *"This'll do for the night till we find where people are stopping."* And we did do.

We pulled on there and there was just us on, but there was no electric - we didn't have no generators or anything then. And the funny thing was - we had mantels on the trailer, but by the time we got from Darlington to Leeds, they'd broke off, so we had no lights. As soon as we had our tea and got washed and everything, we went to bed.

Next morning when we got up and we looked round I thought to meself, *"I don't really like it here."* It was the middle of nowhere - we'd been used to the town - Darlington - right in the middle of the town, 'cos where I was born, you could walk a few hundred yards into the middle of Darlington town centre. We were used to the town and we thought Leeds was a really big town, but when we woke up next morning and looked at this place! I was only a little kid and I thought, *"I don't like it here."* Anyway, someone come to us and he said, *"We're all stopping on the Dog Track. If you follow me up I'll show you where it is."* And that was how we come to go onto the Dog Track.

And when we got up there, there were loads and loads of Travellers, so I thought, *"Oh, it's not too bad."* And that's how it really started, from there, but then when we got moved off from there, we started pulling a lot more round Hunslet, and me Dad used to stop a lot on his own, you know, probably only one or two together, and that's how we come to stop in Hunslet for all them years.

I'd say I was about six years old when I came to Leeds. I remember, a lot about that, it's funny. I don't remember what I did yesterday, but I can remember that. And there was me Mam and Dad and three brothers, and me oldest brother, he's gone back to settle in Darlington. And he's been back there now about eight years. But the rest of us have stayed in Leeds.

Me Dad died about fifteen year ago, and we're all married now, like. So it's another little generation starting up, with the children and their children.

As I say, we come to Leeds and we used to stay up and down the grounds, and then it would be about 30 year ago that they started on about sites, and that's how we first come to go on sites. Me Dad always said that he wouldn't - never go on them places - he'd heared about them, but then when it come to it, there were no other thing to do but to go on to sites, because you just couldn't stay round any more, you know. We were down Hunslet when they finished building that site up there, and the man, it were a Mr. Batty then, used to come round, and he said to me Dad, *"Come on, Bill, this site's lovely up there, what we've got built for you."* There were nobody on it. He said, *"You've to be the caretaker up there."* So we said, *"No, we're not going on,"* and one thing and another, and then one or two pulled on. And then Michael's Mam and Dad went on and then we finally went on, and me Dad then, he was the caretaker for a while up there.

I don't know why things changed, I don't know whether it's something to do with the Council or what, but they got that many Travellers staying around. When we first come to Leeds there wasn't so many. We could even stop behind the pubs and things like that, which we did - we stopped behind the Sun pub in Hunslet there. We stopped there a long while, and the landlord and landlady were really kind to us, and missed us when we went, but as time went on and they got more and more people into Leeds, well there were just too big a Traveller population to do what we used to do. So of course the only other alternative then were sites where they could put 'em all together. And that's what happened. What happened as well, they started building and building and there wasn't the space any more.

This is Great Grandad Georgie Pattison and his wife Janie and family. His brother was known as 'Crying Tommy Pattison', a real character. They are atchin' in a yard in Hartlepool, This was back in 1916 and they were there for years.

Well that old landlord from the pub is still alive now; of course, he's retired, he's old. But I sometimes see him if I go into Leeds and he always asks how all the family is and, you know, really concerned. But he left that pub about fifteen years since, but he was in it a lot of years. That's what really happened here, but it really was, there was that many coming into Leeds and there was just too many people for to carry on like we used to do. Mind, it must have happened everywhere - not only in Leeds - because for how many sites there is all over the country now.

When we first come to Leeds you got stopping for a few weeks. They were really lenient then, they used to come and they'd say, *"Oh, well you can have a couple of weeks."* And then they'd even come back and say again, *"Well you've been alright, there's been no complaints, you haven't left any rubbish - you can have another couple of weeks."* And that's how it went on, but times changed just before the 70's, because I got married in 1970, so, like I was only sixteen then, but it would probably be '67 or '68 when it started to really get bad. They were coming in every, well not even every forty-eight hours - every twenty-four hours - they were coming nearly every day, and you were moved from place to place. Sometimes you didn't even unpack the wagon because they were there next day to move yer.

We didn't hate the people who came to evict us because, as I say, there was one old man, they called him Mr Batty, and Eric the policeman, he used to come on a bike, he were a big fat policeman. And he knowed us all by our names - I should think he did, because he used to come and tell us every day to move. But it were their job, wasn't it? They had to do their jobs, so we had to shift, but no, I didn't hate them for coming to move us. But it got so bad that in the end me Dad used to say, *"Oh no now, this is just getting above it. You'll make people have nervous breakdowns - keep moving 'em on and moving 'em on."* They were a little bit lenient at times, they'd say, *"Well alright then, we'll leave you a couple of days."*

But then, towards the latter end, they used to come round, it was a Landrover. If you said you weren't moving, they used to back on to the trailer move yer themselves, so if you didn't want to risk having your bits of things broke up, you'd had for all them years, you had to move on. It got really bad. That's why we had to go on the sites, that's why we had to go up on that site, because there was just no life. And then we got shifted up and down and the site was already made up there; it was just waiting for people to go on it, take that step. People didn't want to go on it.

And that was why me Dad said, in the end, *"We'll go up on that site. What we'll do, we'll go up and just try it for a week and see what it's like."* Well, that were it, then, once he was up there, he was up there, because he thought to himself then, *"Well, I'm not getting moved."* It was more settling in some ways, but it was the worst thing that, I think, could happen to Travellers, these sites. But, as I say, it had to be, and that were it. Me Dad was the caretaker up there. He was a funny caretaker. He used to reckon to keep it clean and that, and he used to have his rags, you know, all little piles of rags all over, but he was the caretaker and they didn't really bother, they just used to let him carry on.

This was when we were stopping on the new site at Cottingley in 1985.

I think a lot of the Travellers - the sites was too big of a thing for 'em. *"They're going to put us up on them sites and that'll be the end of us."* And really it were true. I think so, anyway, because once people got up there, it were never the same. You didn't have the same freedom as you'd had when you were living how we used to live. I think once you were up there, you were up there, and that was it. It made things worse. And I think it's got worser now on the sites - they've had to pull onto them, they've had to do it for the sake of somewhere to stop. They've even now started putting barriers on 'em, on the sites. You're completely closed in, aren't you, with these barriers. You're not so bad up there, because they don't have 'em down all the time, but on a lot of the sites they do. So you can't get off. Same as that one at Knaresborough, that site, they have that barrier down, and you've got to go and get the key if you're taking a big vehicle in. But it's all done for a reason, it's for people coming on it who hasn't got space, so of course it all has to be done. But it all adds up. I think people feel trapped, like we were on them long enough to get used to 'em really, but I don't think you ever do get used to 'em. No.

Me Dad went to the pub every night at nine o'clock and pubs used to shut at ten o'clock then, didn't they? So they used to go for the last hour every night. Me Mam and me Dad both together. Me Dad went on a little bit in front of her, she used to follow him on then for about quarter past nine. They went out every night in life, until they went up on that site and then after that it all changed. They didn't do it then. They used to go out odd times, but not like they used to do when we were somewhere stopping. But once they got up there they had to have a motor or catch buses, and you couldn't always get a bus back, so it just died out. The sites haven't really worked.

But meself I've settled down now in this little house, and I've found that I should have done this years ago, because, being like you are, if I want to walk to a shop, I can walk to a shop - walk anywhere. When we were up on them sites, you couldn't, because you needed transport to get you everywhere. The site was in the wrong place, if they'd built it in Hunslet, say, it would have been better. The size of the first site was fine, but then they built the new one at the bottom and they built that other one at the back, and of course there were just too many together. They built 'em too close together, they should have split 'em up - it wouldn't have been so bad then, but I don't suppose they'll change it now, will they, because it's cost that much to build 'em and everything.

I've got a poem about it. It's all what happened in my life and me family's life, so it's true, it's really just come from me heart. I've called it **'Changes'**, because I think that's what it is.

That photograph of me grandfather and me grandmother was just before me Dad was born, so that must be seventy-five, seventy-six years old. The other photo's of me great-grandfather George, and me great-granny, Janie. That was when me grandfather was at home, so you can imagine how old that one must be, so it could be ninety-five years old that one. The photo of me grandfather could have been York because I've heard me Granny before she died stayed there. The wagon has a 'P' for Pattison carved in the window.

They did a lot of handicraft in them days, they were very clever people then, they did a lot themselves. Well me dad used to just gather a few rags and a bit of scrap, that's what he used to do. But originally, in his generation, they were tinsmiths, they used to make cans and these jacks and all such as that, all them years ago. But me Dad, he never followed it up. The trade died when the plastic came. And there was really no call for it. If me Dad weren't doing anything, all them years since, then me Mam would go out with a basket, selling a little bit of lace, or a few brushes and combs, just to keep us.

Changes

"They're coming to move us," I heard my Mam say.
"Come on, help your brother, there's no time to play.
Pick up the dishes, the buckets - that pan.
It's there by the fire. Quick, here comes the man."

"We'll give you till 12, then be on your way.
There's no need to argue, you really can't stay.
Move on to the next town." I don't like it here,
It's too close to the road side, of traffic I fear.

"Tie up the old juck or he won't last long."
"Oh, he's olling the rope, Dad, he knows that's wrong.
It's starting to rain. Mam, we'll catch it to use.
Let's fill all the buckets, there's no time to lose."

Night starts to fall now. There's no traffic sound.
We all fall to sooty 'til morning comes round.
A knock on the varda. *"Dad, someone to see."*
A man with a notice - *"Be gone now by three."*

They're building new places. They're calling them sites.
It's a big step to take, but Dad said we might.
"It all sounds so final," Mam starts to say.
"We'll all have to go on them", Dad says, *"some day."*

Travelling is finished and this life is through.
We'll try that new site for a week - maybe two.
But thirty years later them sites they are many.
Our people have changed now, I do not know any.

I'm glad Dad can't see it, but who do we blame?
That man who came knocking, but, what was his name?
There's so many changes - life's never the same.

(Romanes: jukel - dog,   sooty - sleep,   varda - wagon)

This is Grandad Jack Pattison and his wife Ellen with their children Caroline and Dianne together with Lizzy, the servant girl.

This Bill Wright's square topped wagon was specially made for them. You can see the 'P' for Pattison etched on the windows.

Piercing little girls ears, it's something that's gone on for generations, that, with the earrings. Now today, when you look at some of them, and they've got two or three pair in, I think that looks stupid. Sometimes they're done as soon as they're born, as soon as they really come out of hospital they used to have their ears pierced. Mainly their mothers, and their grandmothers do it with a cork and a needle. I had mine done with a cork and a needle. Yes, but when my little lasses were old enough to have their ears done, I wouldn't hear of it. I had proper sterilised things that they put in.

But I had mine done with a needle and a cork. I can remember in Layfields Yard, 'cos me Dad wouldn't let me have mine done till I were about three or four year old. I can remember in Layfields Yard, me Mam and her sister were doing 'em, and they waited while me Dad had gone off to do me ears, because he were, *"Don't you do her ears"*, you know. *"She hasn't got to have needles put in her ears"*. And he'd gone off and I were running round Layfields Yard with one needle and a cork through one ear and the other one not done, trying to put me ear under the tap outside. Me Mam were frightened to death saying, *"If her Father ever comes back he'll kill us."* But anyway they got the other one done. It did hurt. I wouldn't let my lasses have theirs done like that, I said, *"They'll do without earrings if they have to have corks."*

Music was also important. Me Granddad, Jackie, he used to play an accordion and he could make it talk. The music and songs still goes on amongst Travellers but the majority of it now, is at weddings and christenings. But years ago me Dad said his Dad and his grandfather, when they used to be in them Yards at Hartlepool and that, me Granddad, I mean they didn't drink then, they didn't need drink to make them have a good time. After they'd had their supper and they'd washed up, well they'd sit round the fire and they'd play the accordion and even sing but they don't do that today they need a wedding or something.

The ways things are changing now you're going to have to really be educated to get on in this world and a lot of our children, well a lot of it's their own doing, but they haven't had that chance. When we used to stop on the site, we still used to go away some time in the summer, so of course children's been missing out. Where if they'd been in a house settled, like we've been now, and the children had (just let's say my lasses) had had a full education,

I'm sure, although they both got a good job, they had permanent jobs up to them both getting married. It still would have been easier if they'd had that bit better education. They could have had probably a better job. Although they would have still got married at nineteen and that, which is young really. I was sixteen, but, them days it didn't seem as bad, but you know, I often think now that if they'd been able to get more settled, they'd have had a better education.

I think that really about meself as well, and me brothers, I left school, when we come to Leeds from Darlington, so I was only in the Infants. I went to Burrow Road School in Darlington. It's still there now. What would I be, probably six when I left, so the reading I learnt, I learnt in that little bit of time. Never went to school after that. I mean, how could we have gone to school when we were shifted so much? We'd have been going to school one morning, from one place, coming back on a night, and the trailers wouldn't have been there - they'd have been somewhere else. So that was one of the biggest things, really, why we didn't go to school. What I learnt, I learnt meself after that and I passed my test first time, you know.

We didn't go to school but we were busy. The lasses were the 'cleaner-uppers,' I think little lasses, in their own little way, they clean even from such an early age, you know, clean up and help. The lads, when they were younger they'd help me Dad with his few rags, his bit of scrap, to get it ready. Our little George, and the lads when they were younger - what would he be? Five or six? He used to have a little bogey and he'd go look for little bits of scrap. Then they could, but there's nothing about today for 'em to do like that. But I always found something to do. I often wonder now what we did do, what kept us going, but of course we got through it. But I enjoyed me life. We were really happy, but as I say, there have been a lot of changes since then. When I look back now, and look forward to what our little grandchildren, and even theirs, what's it going to be like?

I always wanted to be a nurse, and me poor old Dad, he used to - I used to have a little nurse's uniform and a little hat, and he used to say, *"Come on, take me temperature"* and, *"I've got a headache"*, and all that. Whether it's a stage kids go through, I don't know, but I always wanted to be a nurse. Maybe if I had have had me schooling, I could have probably gone on to be some'at, but I don't know. But I'm a bit old now - forty-two - going to be a nurse. These lasses would take a fit. They'd say, *"Nurse these kids, Mam!"*. I think too much water's gone under the bridge now. Probably if it had been years ago, then I might have done, but no, not now.

This is my Grandad Jack in 1926. He played the accordion and you can see it resting on the place where the water jacks usually stay.

In the past a lot still did marry into non-Travellers, just the same, but I think there's more today, marrying into non-Travellers than what they did years ago. But they did, years ago, they did marry into 'em. But I think there's a lot more today. If a man Traveller married a non-Traveller woman it depended, but most of the time they went into the Traveller's way. They nearly always followed the Traveller's way. And they were accepted by everyone else.

Well, you get the odd ones, you know, *"Look at them; they're not Travellers."* Them who say it should sometimes be the least to talk, but you do, you still get 'em today. *"Well, look at them; they're not Travellers. Who do they think they are?"* But the majority of 'em goes back themselves. There'll be some amongst everybody, which there is, I mean, them old photographs what I've give yer, there's not many that can show their great-grandfather. There's not many that can show them. Not many who'll you go round today can show them. So really you don't know who are Travellers and who are not, right back, because who's to say. You can always pick Travellers out, really - I think so. You can always pick 'em out, but sometimes you can say - *"They're not"* - but a lot of the time you can pick 'em out - who's who. You can pick families out too.

I'm proud of what I am. We've always called ourselves Travellers. In Darlington, where we come from, it was always Travelling people, but when we come to Leeds, they used to say Gypsies. We got called Gypsies when we come to Leeds but when we went to school in Darlington, you did get the odd one that used to call, like they do in Leeds, call you *'Gyppo'*; in Darlington they didn't - it was, *"You're a Traveller, you."* It's funny that, isn't it? It was only when we come to Leeds that we really heard more about *'Gypsy, Gyppo'*, because in Darlington where we fetched up it was, *"You're a Traveller."* So it didn't sound too bad, did it, really? It's the same thing but I would describe myself as a Traveller, I think. If anybody said to me - well they do say it in the street - *"Angela, are you really a Gypsy?"* I say *"Yes"* I don't hide it. And they say to me even me neighbours and that, *"Well you wouldn't think so."* *"Well, what would you think that I am?"* *"Well, I don't know, but not a Gypsy."* You know, as if Gypsies are a bad thing when they're not really are they?

We have our own language but it's getting more used and used amongst everybody now. If you put the television on - I know a lot of it is not Romanes and it's slang, but a lot of the Travellers will use slang as well as Romanes. But you put your television on, Brookside and all these things, and many a time, I kill myself with laughing, because they talk it all the time. You learn it by hearing it off your Mam and Dad, certain things, and I mean, like, when they say *"muskras"*, everybody knows what muskras is now, don't they?

When you were a little kid and used to say, as you got older, *"The muskras is here."* And then, when you went to school, I can remember our Joanne when she went up to that school at Belle Isle, and they come in the yard, the policemen. They come into the schoolyard and she were in class and she was saying, *"The muskras is here."* They were all looking at her - whatever is she on about? And like when she come home from school and she told me, she said, *"The muskras have been in our yard, Mam, and nobody knowed who they was."*

But now it's used a lot - Romanes slang amongst everybody, so there's not really much you can say in front of anybody that they don't know anyway. Times has moved on, but years ago, the older people, not me or mine, but say like them you've got on them photographs, they could talk to each other about everything and nobody would know a word they were saying, but today it's a different thing. It's used by every walk of life.

When I look at me grandsons, I just hope really they go on like their fathers do, their Dads, you know, they go out and do the best they can, they don't do anything what they shouldn't do, they go out and earn it honest, and I just hope it carries on for me grandsons, and me own little lad. What it all boils down to it has changed, it really has changed a lot. What's going on today to what went on even ten year ago. These little 'uns, now, running about, these is the new generation. They're going to find it hard, really.

I mean, we used to stop up and down Hunslet; we had no taps, but it was easy then, because we could go - if we wasn't outside the back of the pub there, we'd be somewhere along Hunslet Road. We could still come to any of these pubs, get a can of water, and we could get it anywhere 'cos we were well known. But as time went on, and a lot got round, they wouldn't give 'em water. *"No I'm not giving the Gypsies no water. Go to the garage."* Started going to the garage, then the garage - probably sometimes let you have it and other times, *"No, we're not giving you none."* It all added to having to go up on that site.

This is our Joanne and Tracey with their cousins Lavinia Pattison and Andra and Levi Pattison and Henry Heron. They were on a day out to Ilkley Moor with Travellers Education Service and were having a good time. This is when they were only small back in 1982.

I think everybody gets on with everybody, Traveller and non-Traveller. Like me here with all the people in the street. They've all accepted us. They know what we are, where we're from, and they'll even joke on. I've got a barbecue there what I do the kids a bit of barbecue on, and they'll put their heads over the fence, *"Oh she thinks she's back up on the site."* I laugh, you know. *"Have you got any spare there, Angie?"* If I have I'll offer them. So they've accepted us.

I was worried about them accepting us before we came here. I thought how are they going to react to us, because, I mean, it wasn't just me and me husband and me little lad coming down here, because when my lasses come, and your brothers come, you can always tell what we are. You know what I mean? They don't just come in cars, so people don't know whose who. They all know. They say, *"They're definitely Travellers these - look at them."* So of course, everybody in the street knows exactly what we are, where we're from, and there's been no criticism whatsoever. It's really good. Because I've been here two years. Everybody's been really fine with us.

We come into this house new which helped and we all come together, so everyone was coming to a new little community together, and they were all wondering who they was going to get next door. I think a lot of 'em thought to theirselves, *"Oh, these are Travellers. What they gonna be like?"* And they found out that we were just the same as them. And every one of them is lovely with us. They'll knock on the door and say, *"Can I bring you anything from the shop, Angie?"* or, *"If you're going anywhere, do you want to leave Michael with us?"* So they're very helpful and I've no regrets whatsoever of coming down here, and living down here. I love it. I'll never go back.

This is me and Michael, my son, at Claire Buxton's and David Wilkinson's wedding in Leeds in 1992. A wedding is always a happy occasion and it is a great time for everyone to get together.

Appleby Charter Fair

EARLY ORIGINS

In 1685, King James II gave Appleby-in-Westmorland, a charter allowing a horse fair to be held each year on a site near the river Eden.

Gypsies and Travellers have been coming to Appleby all these years and have kept this traditional horse fair alive. It is the one place where families can meet their friends and relations. It is a social gathering as much as a fair.

The Fair attracts thousands of people every year and most Gypsies and Travellers pull their trailers or wagons onto Fair Hill.

The Fair lasts five days in all and takes place in June. Everyone pulls on the weekend before the second Wednesday in June, which is the final day.

APPLEBY REMEMBERED

Everyone used to go. There were very few motors - everyone had wagons and horses. You'd always see someone on the road and you used to travel up together. From Hartlepool - a hundred miles - it took three or four days. We used to pull on the hill.

We'd pull in on Saturday or Sunday and had to be off on the Thursday.

The first day of Appleby on the Tuesday was in the middle of the town and the second day, Wednesday, was on the top of the hill.

I never missed it. It were a change. Them days you didn't need a lot of money to buy a horse. If you had twenty pounds you were a rich man. We'd buy and sell horses, swap 'em. There used to be singing and dances around the fires.

Tom Kendall

- past and present

HORSES AND WAGONS

The trading of horses has changed little over the centuries and takes place in a country lane, an old Roman road, above Fair Hill. The horses are washed in the river Eden in Appleby town and then taken up onto the hill to be sold.

APPLEBY WAGONS

This is Billy Gentle, me Uncle, from Newcastle. He's in his open lot on Appleby top with his great nephew and niece, Yogi and Star. They were up from Leeds for The Fair, in 1981.

Ede Smith

DUKKERING AT THE FAIR

Telling Fortunes - it's a thing, little bits of things you pick up. But you're born with it. You can tell so much, so much you can't. It's a little gift...
Shirley Lee

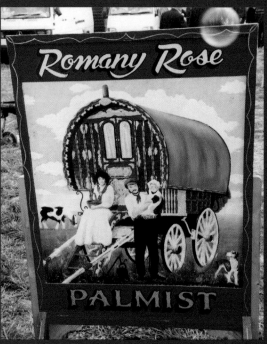

They used to go 'Dukkering' - doing 'Fortune Telling'. It's a thing that would be handed down from centuries and centuries. God knows where it comes from.
Sakie Lee

IT'S A LITTLE GIFT...

This is me Mam, Ada Gray, telling the Lord Mayor of Dublin's fortune in 1986. Me Mam always went to Appleby every year with all her family, the Gentles. They never miss it. She's been telling fortunes since she was twelve years old.

Ede Smith

Appleby Charter Fair

LOWTHER FAMILY MEMORIES FROM KAY JAMES

This is me Mam, Nellie Lowther with her friends Violet Robshaw and Dinah Hamshaw on Appleby Fair in the 40's. They are wearing pinnies which they wore in them days.

You can see the bow top wagons behind them. They used to travel up from Leeds in them and it took about four days. They'd stop at Wetherby, Scotch Corner, Smallways and Brough before pulling into Appleby for the Fair.

These are my nieces Caroline and Ellen Louise Lowther and Ellen Batt. This was taken on Appleby in 1970. We always used to pull on the hill every year and they had come through from Leeds visiting for the day.

This was taken on Appleby Trots in 1965 when I was 12.

I'm with me Mam, Nellie Lowther, Rocky and Jimmy Adams, Shane and Alfie Robinson, Black Johnny Tyres, and Alice Pop.

We went shopping and looking round the stalls.

- a family meeting place

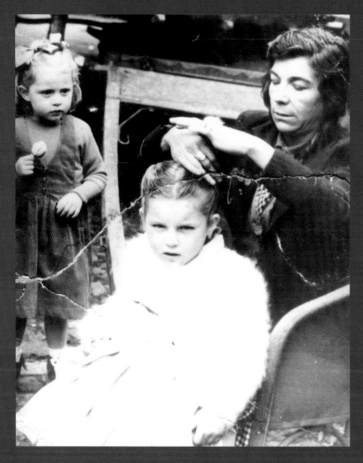

An old rakli doin' the little rakli's bal to make her look kushti.

Dik at the goodla pover in the tikna's vast.
(Romanes)

Lizzie Francis, me sister, doin' Betty Blue's hair back in the fifties.

You can see the shafts of the rully behind them. It was all horses and wagons, accommodations and carts and square tents in those days.

Sittin' round the yog makin' the hobin for the chors to come home. (Romanes)

This is me mam, Mary Ann Kendal, and me aunt, Margaret Foster, cookin' the food for the boys comin' home from hawkin'.

In one pot there'd be the meat gettin' stewed - a stew roast - and the vegetables would be in the other pot. They would both be hangin' on the kettle props.

This was at the fair back in the sixties.

Appleby Charter Fair

This is Lol Bainbridge with Coral, his daughter and Edna; Caroline Bainbridge with their son Richard; Ann Harker with niece Annie; Kizzy Gaskin with her two children, Billy and Violet; and my children, Annie, Kay, Sally and Henry with their cousins Peter and Robert Harker.

Tommy Gaskin, in the hat, made this wagon for his grandson, Davie Foster, Mandie's Davie. It was a miniature open lot for the children. There's Tom Farrow, Annie Harker and Jimmy Riley with Annie Farrow.

Lucy Farrow and me with the children.

Samboy Riley, Joe Farrar, Jacob Foster and me own daughter, Kay Harker, all having their photo took with the donkey foal on the field at Appleby.

- traditions continue

This is me and Righteous with our Dawn, Lisa, Bullerman and friends on Appleby Fair back in summer 1985.

Linda Price

This is Sonny with Kags and Donna, looking after the stall on Appleby Fair for us in 1992.

Mags Price

Treasured Memories

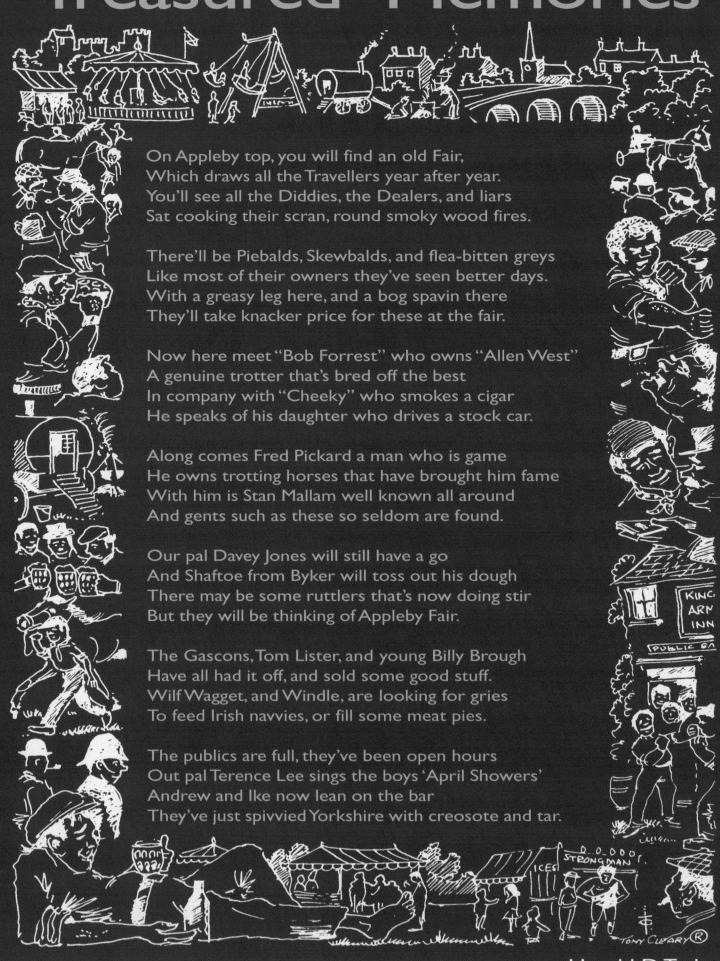

On Appleby top, you will find an old Fair,
Which draws all the Travellers year after year.
You'll see all the Diddies, the Dealers, and liars
Sat cooking their scran, round smoky wood fires.

There'll be Piebalds, Skewbalds, and flea-bitten greys
Like most of their owners they've seen better days.
With a greasy leg here, and a bog spavin there
They'll take knacker price for these at the fair.

Now here meet "Bob Forrest" who owns "Allen West"
A genuine trotter that's bred off the best
In company with "Cheeky" who smokes a cigar
He speaks of his daughter who drives a stock car.

Along comes Fred Pickard a man who is game
He owns trotting horses that have brought him fame
With him is Stan Mallam well known all around
And gents such as these so seldom are found.

Our pal Davey Jones will still have a go
And Shaftoe from Byker will toss out his dough
There may be some ruttlers that's now doing stir
But they will be thinking of Appleby Fair.

The Gascons, Tom Lister, and young Billy Brough
Have all had it off, and sold some good stuff.
Wilf Wagget, and Windle, are looking for gries
To feed Irish navvies, or fill some meat pies.

The publics are full, they've been open hours
Out pal Terence Lee sings the boys 'April Showers'
Andrew and Ike now lean on the bar
They've just spivvied Yorkshire with creosote and tar.

Harold D. Taylor

204

- of Appleby Fair

There must be some trouble for in comes a cop
A man's had a scut with an old kettle prop
But no one says nothing, for Travellers won't talk
And the culprit is missing, he's half-way to York.

Paddy Murphy from Preston is spinning his cracks
While Billy Hill's quoting the price of old sacks
So what with the stack sheets and second-hand bags
No one is bothered about the old Nags.

Larry Howard the chanter now sings to Joe Brown
Who sups all the whiskey that's inside the town
So "order" is given through the length of the bar
While Larry bursts forth with "Master Ma'Gra."

Gold earrings and watch chains gleam in the light
And a man over eighty is wanting to fight
A bloke selling laces is sorting his cash
As he wipes the froth off the ends of his tash.

With all due respect through the course of the day
We drink to old timers, who've now passed away
T'was only by them this Fair was kept going
And thanks to these lads, every Traveller is owing.

Each time the door opens you smell the wood fires
And it's time for a song from young "Sonny Tyers"
"So it's my Mother's Birthday" that now fills the air
And every one's happy at "Appleby Fair".

From the highways and byways the clans have now met
So win, lose, or draw, no one will fret
It's been a great pleasure to put them to verse
You'll never see better, but often meet worse.

June, 1954

205

Appleby Charter Fair

1969

They are having their horse shoed at Appleby. They're holding it at the head and the tail to steady it and let the blacksmith get on with the job.

Tom Kendal

He's taking the horse in the river at Appleby to wash it and cool it down. They've been doing this for hundreds of years.

Tom Kendal

- seen by Dave Thomas

1970

Keith Mounsey from Darlington, he's running his horse on to show it. It's a spotted piebald.

Tom Kendal

Jimmy Shields from Spennymoor. He's showing the horse to sell it. It's a trotting horse with a trotting sulkie for racing.

Tom Kendal

Appleby Charter Fair

1970

A family getting the dinner ready sat round a stick fire with an open lot and homemade bow top at the back.

Tom Kendal

Henry Gaskin

A WELL-LIKED MAN

Me Dad, Henry Gaskin, never missed Appleby in his life, never missed it. He's been goin' since he was a child. He liked the horses and seeing his old pals. He used to travel up with the wagon and the horses and carts. It took about a week from Doncaster, stopping on camps and the roadside. He was a well-liked man and he's missed.

Mary Lowther

Arthur Hamshaw

I'm Arthur Hamshaw and I was born in 1912, 8th October, the year the Titanic went down. So, if it's 1999 now, then I'll be eighty-seven years old on me birthday of this year.

...a few thoughts in words

When I was young, I used to go to me Uncle's. He had a set of roundabouts, seat roundabouts that they used to travel round with. He used to take us away to Doncaster, Bentley. Through the week, when there was no money about, he used to go out for jars and woollens. Me Uncle had a stable at Cravens Yard, and he used to pull the 'willygigs' up in the top end. There were a few stables in the yard. Chip hawkers were there. Billy Brad, he used to go round selling chips, 2d (two old pennies) a bucket.

I got in with Dinah's brother-in-law and I used to go with him, bit of horse trade, allotment holders and such as that, selling 'em small ponies. That's how we met, me wife Dinah and me. I used to go with her father to cut grass, but nobody knew, they hadn't the slightest inclination about us. It was all secret.

I was only young when I got married to my wife. She was four year older than me. And everybody thought it would be a disaster, 'cos it was mixed you see, I was a householder and she was a Gypsy born, but it turned out better than ever. Everyone thought there'd be murder, 'cos her father was very strict. They said, *"Her father'll kill you!"* But he never made a bit of a thing, and we got married in 1930, at Whitsuntide, at Bramley Town End.

The mother come, and aunt, and said, *"You've done a nice trick now, haven't you? What can he do? All he knows is work."* She said, *"Well, I'm satisfied and he's satisfied, so that's it."*

And her father gave me a wagon, what they used to make them days - at Bill Wright's - William Wright's, Rothwell. And he said to me, *"Get a top put on that, Arthur, and it'll make a right good wagon",* which it did. Beautiful, worth £10,000 or £12,000 today, 'cos it were all cut and carved. The dray itself was all on spindles and it had lion heads all the way round it, even on the forecarriage.

Dinah's uncle, Richard James, got the Military Medal in The First World War. One of his mates was shot and he went out and got him. I remember reading it in 'The 'Post' about 'Armley man dies - Richard James receives Military Cross for gallantry'. He was a do and die merchant annorl. I could believe he'd do it - he'd no fear o' nowt. He wasn't much bigger than me, but broad. He'd be about five foot three or four tall, but as strong as a lion. And I could imagine him doing it - when one of his mates was shot he went out and fetched him back again. It doesn't tell lies when they're giving him a Military Medal, does it?

My wife's family used to travel about a bit but they were only away from Leeds for a couple of month and then they were always back. They were in a yard in Leeds, Craven's Yard, from the First World War right up to 1933 when we had to come out.

We stopped in the country lanes for the first two years I was married (1930-32). Summer time it was beautiful, I was in another world. We used to go out through t'day, come back home four o'clock, get us teas and just wander up and down anywhere. Go swimming - we used to stop in a little paddock at Collingham, about ten miles out of Leeds and there was a river running through it, we used to jump in there and swim up and down it. They called 'em Railway Lane because it had the railway running through it, that was six or seven mile out of Wetherby.

This kushti varda was taken on 'The Brickfields', opposite Armley Park in 1933. It is a Bill Wright's bow top. My wife's mother Ann Smith is sitting on the right next to Janie Cunningham. Nellie Wilson is stood inside the wagon.

And there was Yarm Back Lane in Yarm and I've stopped in Sandy Lee Lane, Stockton. They called one Loose Barn Lane, recognised it as that and they all knew where Loose Barn Lane was, everybody what were travelling up and down. That was on the York Road somewhere just past the Fox and Grapes pub before you turn for Barwick. They had names for all t'bits o'places where they stopped.

It's the best life you can have in a sense but it's not good today because you get hounded.

I really gave up travelling, 1936 or 1937, I took houses. Then I came out (of houses) in 1962 owing t'wife's health. The doctor said, *"I'm fearing the worst. Depression. She's left too long on her own because you are working too long. She'll be better in a caravan where she can see round and that, so that's the advice I can give you".* So Monday morning I went straight into work and gave my notice in and I left, I'd been there nearly fifteen years.

I bought this second hand caravan. I got a job with Shepperd's in 1967, as a watchman and I went all over with 'em: University, Park Lane College, Trust Houses at Bramhope living in the caravan and watching the sites. This caravan is thirty year old and it hasn't done five hundred miles. From Leeds to Wakefield, Leeds to Bramhope, University, Bradford, twice at Wakefield. I gave it up in 1984 I said to them, *"Me wife she's not in a fit state to be on t'building sites now, isn't my wife".*

Me wife used to tell me that if she and her sisters were sat round the fire and if any men come round at all, her father just used to look at them like and he used to say to the youngest, *"Can't you go find something to do?"* He'd no need to tell the other sisters, 'cos as soon as they saw his eyes they picked themselves up and off they went away. He wouldn't have men round.

Appleby Fair in the 1930's - it was nearly all wagons, very few trailers, very few. There weren't half a dozen trailer caravans on then. All horse wagons - come from all over Britain, Scotland, London, Wales, and Ireland they did. It was a nice sight in them days. We were all out camping on the road then, today it's different altogether, they're all in the fields. Appleby Fair is touchable, but if you have a rainy Appleby, if it's a bad Appleby they had to 'hook on' to pull 'em out of the mud. That were bad.

Every year they want to do away with it and eventually I think they will get it done away with, I think, 'cos Yarm Fair were a Chartered Fair and they've done away with that and I believe Appleby is a Chartered Fair too.

I haven't been up to Appleby, not to stop since 1963 but I've gone up with t'motor for t'day. We used to go to Ripon Races for a week, that were a nice week there were Ripon races 'cos it was July.

When people died they used to burn the wagons. This'll (trailer) get burnt definitely. We went to a funeral in Darlington, I bet there were 1500 people there, or more and you never seen a funeral in your life like it. It was a niece of my wife. Her husband had a casket for her, had great big handles on it, you couldn't grip the handles. And with her being small, it were made larger, nicest thing I've seen for anybody it was.

Well, I'll be honest with you, I feel safer in here, in me trailer, than I do in a house. In here I can see everybody coming, can't I? Harry down there said to me, *"Why don't you get a house or a flat?"* I said, *"Harry, am I in your way?"* He said, *"No, but I would"*.

I said, *"I can look through t'window to see who's there first, whether it's dark or light and I don't open t'door do I?"* When you're in a house you go innocently and open the door and bang you're on the floor dead.

It's fourteen years since I've been here, on and off. With having a good character, the council man said he wouldn't shift me no more. I've been in Holbeck all me life. Holbeck born and I hope to finish my days here.

The Smith Family

Me father, Little Willie Smith and me Uncle Snicky.

This was taken at Appleby Fair in 1985.

They were both there with my two daughters, Kathleen and Chantelle.

Me father deals in horses and he used to meet up with his brother in Appleby. They used to deal in horses from when they were in Ireland, like their father before them. The horse is a blue and white piebald.

This was taken when we were on Newcastle Town Moor in 1985.

I took the children out for a ride around on me Daddy's flat cart.

They used to use these in Ireland them days for going out hawking - for buying and selling all the old swag.

215

Barry and Gloria

Gloria and I were both born in Leeds, in the late forties. I used to work on the Fairs when I was a child. I travelled all over with the Fair people in them days.

Smith ... about their lives

You get to know where people's stopping, so you go pull to 'em. Like when we used to come to Leeds we used to go to Belle Isle or a place called the 'Lemmy' at Holbeck. We used to go to Belle Isle because there was always a big field there, common land, you could pull in and there was always somebody on Belle Isle at one time. Or the 'Lemmy' there was always people on the Lemmy, there was always trailers - always somebody stopping on there. So you knew to go. Well they've built on the Lemmy now and Belle Isle's all been tree'd.

You'd get a month or so. After a month or six weeks you'd had enough anyhow, so you were ready for shifting. Nobody wanted you - what Travellers'd like to do was pull out of the way somewhere, down an old back tip or where people weren't living in the street houses, you could pull in the old streets, somewhere out of the way where people couldn't see you. If people couldn't see you they wouldn't complain. If they complained they'd shift you.   (Barry)

The council man wasn't too bad. You could talk to him and he'd leave you say another week or so but then you had to be off. Sometimes he might tell you where to go - you know what I mean - where you could go. But as years went on it got worse and worse. I've seen them come one morning and ask you to shift the same day. I've seen us shift every day for weeks.   (Gloria)

We used to go up north a lot, Newcastle, Leyburn. You could stop anywhere. You wasn't hounded as much were you? I wouldn't say travelling days are finished but they're not like they used to be. I think it will finish in another forty or fifty years time. I don't think there'll be a lot of travelling about. You don't see many horses and wagons now do you? I can't remember seeing one for years. It was always wagons. It's all motors now isn't it? They're all in motor caravans, caravanette things aren't they? You get families buying them now. You've got your motor and trailer all in one haven't you?   (Barry)

Nowadays you can't stop you see, they put mounds of earth or they dig ditches or they put stones or blocks in so that you can't pull your trailer on. They make it so that it's near enough impossible to get on. That's why people go on sites because there's nowhere to stop now. They should have places to stop, what you call transit sites what they can just pull on to, have a week or two and then move on if they want to move on; if they want to stop another week or two, stop. But there's none of that. It's all cramming together on sites now. On the camps, we helped one another. If somebody were broke down he could go out with me for a day or two until they got their motor fixed. But I think the sites have stopped travelling, I think they've put travelling back a lot.   (Barry)

When you were working on the fairgrounds you had to work in all weathers. If it were raining you still had to put up and pull down. It was frosty, cold and wet and everything, but it was a way of earning money.

After I was married I got a living just gathering scrap. We cleaned it first, what you call the 'jewellery', the bit of copper and lead and brass and what have you. Then you sorted out the brass and copper and lead and then took that to the scrap yard and weighed that in. It was very hard, you did make a living - just.

It wasn't a good living though by any means. It's a lot harder now, because everything's modern. Everything's plastic - plastic guttering and plastic fall piping, you don't get the old iron fall pipes.   (Barry)

We couldn't get a new trailer because the children were too busy getting married. Me husband was just working for weddings. When mine got married, one after another were getting married, in three years four of 'em got married. All he worked for was wedding cake!   (Gloria)

I've had a few horses. You don't get 'em like you used to. Travellers used horses to get their living, to go out with but now they've got motors, so many Travellers haven't got horses but what horses they've got, they like a nice horse for the simple reason - why keep a bad 'un when you can keep a good 'un? They still take as much to keep so you might as well keep a good 'un.   (Barry)

Crown Derby's the best, so if you like the best - it's the same as having a horse. You might as well have a good horse as a bad horse. So you have good china instead of bad china.   (Barry)

Older people like Crown Derby, I like it myself but a lot of young 'uns today don't want it. I've got one daughter doesn't entertain Crown Derby, doesn't like it at all. She has plates and all that but she won't put it up, she'd rather have these little Coleport figures. And my other daughter she loves it, can't get enough of it. You know what you buy the Crown Derby and jewellery for? - to leave it to your kids. That's what it is, when I die mine will go to my kids.   (Gloria)

Travelling people get blamed for a lot of things they don't do you know. If they don't know who to blame it on, they blame it on the Travellers. If there are some Travellers stopping in a town and something goes off what they don't know who's done it, *"Oh Travellers will have done it, Gypsies will have done it"*. There used to be signs on the doors **'No caravan dwellers'**. Now, the signs have come down but they don't want you in do they?   (Barry)

I think what it used to be with a lot of people in houses and that, they thought 'cos we were staying somewhere on a bit of old ground we were living free, it didn't cost us nowt only a bottle of gas, but they'd to pay. We still have to feed and clothe and wash ourselves. They can turn a tap on and get water, we couldn't, we had to go get water. They could turn their tap on and get a wash and a bath. If I wanted a bath I had to go to the local baths or get a strip wash in a dish. We used to go to garages and get water in milk churns. I've seen us go five or six miles for water and that costs - that wants petrol and oil and diesel in and tax and insuring. We had to pay for battery charging.   (Gloria and Barry)

Years ago we didn't have generators - we just had black and white telly on a battery and gas lights in the trailer. We had no electric at all. So you really liked it (on the site) because you'd got electrical things. But as years went on it got worse and worse (on the road), so you had to be on the site.   (Gloria)

I can see it being a lot worse when my grandchildren grow up. What are their lives going to be like when they're grown up and married? I wouldn't like to be their age now to grow up. I'm glad I've had my time travelling about but they've got all theirs to come, haven't they? And what's it going to be like?

I think eventually everybody will be in houses - it'll take a long time but gradually it will get that way. More and more people is getting houses now than has ever got houses.

It's took all the fun and enjoyment out of travelling, it used to be lovely travelling up and down from town to town.   (Gloria)

Outside the trailer on Cottingley site, 1997.

The Nicholson Family

BIG JIM'S RECOLLECTIONS

These are real old photographs of me Mam Joanne Winter, and her Mam Mary, with my aunties. It was taken in Cumberland years ago, just before the Great War of 1914-18. You can see the wagon behind them.

This is the Winter family with Mary Winter, me Granny, with a scarf and shawl and all me uncles and aunties, the Nicholsons.

- Big Jim looking back

BIG JIM'S RECOLLECTIONS

This is a photo of me Dad, Isaac William Nicholson, with me brother Isaac at Tow Law in 1924, just before I was born. Me Dad was a great man, who travelled all his life dealing in horses.

I was born on 4th June 1925 and I've been going to Appleby Fair all these years.

I was born at 'Tow Law', Walsingham, in County Durham just before the time of Appleby Fair.

This is me Mam, Joanne Nicholson, with me wife Katie and family in front of me Mam's Heron wagon from Hartlepool. It was when the children were small.

This is me brother Robert with me son, Bimbo, took at Ulverston. We had a Heron wagon and an old Crofts lorry from West Hartlepool. We were always travelling and we'd stop for a few weeks and then move on.

This is me brother Isaac with me son Bimbo in 1955. We had a Whitaker and Hutchinson wagon from Bradford and we were stoppin' at Ashington in Northumberland.

- in the 1950's and 60's

BIG JIM'S RECOLLECTIONS

These are me brothers, Isaac and Robert. We were camping in Glasgow with the wagon and horses - no motors them days. The horses all got loose on Christmas Eve and we rounded them up. This was 1956.

We were camping in the main street at Yarm where we were goin' for the fair in 1960.

I've got a Fred Hill wagon which was made in Swinefleet, in Lincolnshire.

There is Jimmy and Biddy Mulvanney, my sister, Marina, and me and Katie with the children, Henry, Kizzy and Isabel.

The Nicholson Family

This is me wife, Katie, taken in 1968 at Appleby Horse fair. We went every year and had lots of great times.

It was better days altogether, it was easier living, we could stay anywhere and no one used to bother us. The sites have ruined it 'cos you can't stay anywhere now.

This is Jimmy Berry, me and Jimmy Mannion in a Public in Appleby in the eighties. Jimmy Berry was a great friend and two of his daughters married two of my brothers.

- still growing in number

This is me and Katie in 1982. We were stopping in Leeds on a big ground in Thorpe. One of me grandaughters, Esther Rose, had just been born.

We were at East Ardsley, Leeds, camping in a big field. My Kizzy and Isabel are with all me grandchildren. This was in 1982. Now I've got over seventy grandchildren and great grandchildren.

Margaret Connors

My name is Margaret Connors and I was born in Bradford, St. Lukes Hospital, in 1980.

...memories of recent times

My earliest memory is of when we were living in Domestic Street, Leeds. We used to make doll's houses and play 'hide and seek' all around the camp. Later on, I had to keep an eye on the children and do some work around the camp. Wash up, clean around the trailer, do the floor, tidy it all up like.

We've been to other places, but we've always stayed around Leeds. We stayed around Manchester at one time, but we were getting shifted nearly every day or every second day. We were always shifting every minute. We'd maybe pull on one day and the next day they'd be there to shift us on again.

You would, like, be all mixed. People you would know. Family and all different Travellers together. You'd be all in the one place but the ones that know each other would be all up the one end in their own group.

Me Daddy decided where we shifted. When we'd pull on to one camp and he'd know we'd have to shift, he'd go and look for another camp to pull on, for when we'd have to pull off the other one.

You'd get longer then on a camp (ten years ago) but now you only get maybe a few days - three or four days. But then you'd maybe get a week, two weeks, maybe more.

I knew everyone on here when I came on to Cottingley site because I knew them all before that. I used to stay with them in other places, so it was no different really, because I knew everyone on here. The difference was, it's handier, isn't it? The site's only really a steady place where you stay, you don't have to leave every day. You don't have to worry about being dragged out in the morning or whatever. On a camp where you pull in one day and you think about having to shift the next day. On a site you don't think about that, do you? But on a camp there's usually shops all round you and all, where here, on the site, it must be two miles to a shop.

Boys can just get up and go on about their business. Me brother gets up in the morning and he goes off on the bike and he'll be gone all day, and nothing be said to him, because he's a boy. We're (girls) allowed to go some places, like pictures and places but we have to clean up and do everything first.

The other children, they'd notice how we talked different. They'd know even before that we were Travellers and they didn't used to call us Travellers, they used to call us Gypsies. I told them we weren't Gypsies we were Travellers. To them Gypsies and Travellers, it's all the one isn't it?

Me Granddad Jimmy Connors, with friends and family, years ago.

This is me Great Granddaddy Mickey Connors, or 'Old Pop' as he was known. Me Granddaddy, Jimmy Connors, is in the middle with his sister, Mary McCann. This was taken back in 1955 at a camp on some spare ground at Toll Bar, Bentley, in Doncaster.

These are me mother's people, years ago in Ireland, my granny's aunts and uncles, the Murphys.

That's me Daddy's brother and sisters and his Mammy and Daddy taken when they were stoppin' in Liverpool in 1966.

This is me old Ma and me old Da givin' the horse a drink.

Billy, me cousin, is sittin' on the horse's back.

This was on a camp in Hunslet in 1983.

Me Mammy and Daddy's Wedding Day. This was in January 1979 at St. Patrick's Church, Leeds.

This is a good mollie in Leeds for the gaulyers to play on.

(Cant)

This was took in Meanwood in 1985. It was a good summer camp and we got stoppin' for a few weeks.

EARLY DAYS ON CAMP

This is me, next to 'Jim Jim' on his donkey and me Daddy. We were on a camp in Leeds in 1983.

Me Daddy with Jim Jim and Poochie on the cart and Christie Sweeney holding the horse's harness.

We were on a camp in Belle Isle, Leeds in 1985.

All Catholic Travellers believe in Holy Communion. So it's important to Catholic Travelling people that their children make their First Holy Communion and then, when you're a bit older, your Confirmation.

For your Holy Communion you get a dress and a veil and rosary beads. The priest comes out and the nuns and they give you tapes to learn off, like all little prayers on the tapes. Sister Ann used to come out on to the top site when I was making my Holy Communion and she used to bring these little tapes out that we could learn off. You have to learn all the prayers, the important prayers, the Act of Contrition and all things like that.

Travellers do have very big weddings. Travellers' weddings are not like invitation weddings. When you have a wedding, anyone can come - all Travellers can just come. Whenever anyone hears of a wedding - 'Oh, there's a wedding. I'm going, I'm going, are you going?' And all rushing to get there.

Me and my family in our trailer in 1989 when I was small.

Me old Ma, Michelle, me Mammy and me gettin ready for Danny's party.

We were stoppin' on Halton Moor in Cross Green. We were havin' a party for Dan's third birthday in 1992. There's Doll Dolls, Dan, me, me Daddy, Michael, Johnboy and Brian Joyce at the back.

Cottingley Springs Caravan Sites

The original Cottingley Springs Caravan Site was the first 'Official' site for Travellers built by Leeds City Council in 1969. It was a response to the Caravan Sites Act 1968 which made it the responsibility of every local authority to provide sites for those Travellers that "reside or resort to their area".

The minimum provision was for fifteen caravans, which is what Leeds provided. At that time there were two hundred and twenty-five caravans in Leeds.

In return for their weekly rent, the residents enjoyed security of tenure and would not be moved on. The 'official' site provided individual plots of hardstanding, each with an elecricity supply and postal service. There were shared drinking water and toilet facilities and refuse collection from skips which were provided.

Most families continued to live on the roadside or on pieces of waste ground. Families lived without any water, sanitation, hardstanding, postal delivery or rubbish collection. These families were continually moved on and found access to education and health care very difficult.

COTTINGLEY SPRINGS OFFICIAL SITE, 1969
The council built this site and at last our families had somewhere to stop without being shifted all the time. This was the beginning of site provision in Leeds. It came about 'cos we had campaigned hard for them to do something for us here.

Tommy Doherty

COTTINGLEY SPRINGS

COUNCIL PROVISION

The First Official Site in Leeds

Things seemed to be better in 1983, being young. There was no worries, we would just play about on a motorbike or bike or something. Aldy, me cousin, was always with us and he used to pal about with me all the time. I was only about ten and the site was alright. It was better than stoppin' on the grounds at least there was water and electric. That's me, me brother Sean, and me cousin Aldy.

Michael Price

This was taken in 1984 on the old site at Cottingley Springs. It was called the 'Top Site' when the new one was built in 1987. There is our Star with her cousins, Tracey and Mileta and Kay Kay James. We all lived on there for years and it was a happy time when the kids were small.

Ede Smith

This was taken in 1986 when our Anne Marie was a baby. We were stopping on Cottingley Springs, on the 'old site', up on the hill. There is Mandy with his dog, 'Blue', Joseph, holding Anne Marie, Kathleen and Eileen with Mileta. We were living on there for years and it was alright, everyone got on well together.

Eileen Lowther

IN THE 1980's

Cottingley Springs New Site

In 1987 Cottingley Springs New Site was built for a further twenty families. This was a good site in that all the families had their own plot with their own facilities in a utility block including, a washroom, bathroom, toilet and electric point for the trailer.

The old site was refurbished with toilets for each plotholder, built in blocks on the site. This was a temporary measure whilst plans were made for further council provision.

AERIAL PHOTOGRAPH OF THE ORIGINAL COTTINGLEY SPRINGS 'OLD' SITE AND ABOVE IT THE 'NEW' SITE BEING BUILT.

I stopped on the old site for a few years. It was a temporary transit site whilst we were waiting for the new site at the bottom to be ready.

When we moved down we were delighted to have all new facilities, it was a big step forward.

We were all grateful to the Council and the people who helped and got this site organised.

We are still on it and have been here twelve years.

Bill Doran

COTTINGLEY 'NEW' SITE

COUNCIL PROVISION

Two Sites at Cottingley Springs

The new site had just opened and we've all moved down from the Top Site. You can see the new fences and sheds, it was really good!

There's Davie, Danny, Rosemarie, Joanne and Michael, Kathleen and Anne Marie, Jobie, Jo Jo, Star and Henry.

Ede Smith

COTTINGLEY SPRINGS 1988

*This shows the old 'Top Site' up the lane and the new one at the bottom.
The old one was alright, but there was no proper facilities. There was only a tap and electric. The toilets you had to share with everybody.*   Ede Smith

COTTINGLEY SPRINGS 1988

Cottingley Springs New Site

THIS IS COTTINGLEY SPRINGS NEW SITE, FIRST BUILT IN 1987

It's a good site with all your own amenities on the slabs. It's not too big a site either. You can see the blue Nursery Bus visiting for the young children.

COTTINGLEY NEW SITE 1988

COUNCIL PROVISION

Cottingley Springs 'New' Becomes 'A'

CHILDREN AND HORSE IN 1998 ON COTTINGLEY SPRINGS 'A' SITE

This is Peter with all the children, Chantel, Leonie, Shona, May, Anne-Marie and Ben, Kizzy holding the horse, and little Peter, our Grandson, riding the horse. Peter and Lee had been washing out the horse and sorting it out. They were giving everyone a ride round the site. We've always kept horses, it's a bit of a hobby and Peter breeds them. We were all brought up with horses, and it's tradition, they just follow on with them.

Kay James

In 1990, another site was built at Cottingley Springs for thirty-six families and it was called Cottingley 'B' site. The old 'Top Site' was closed. The second site, built in 1987, at the bottom of the hill, was now called 'Cottingley Springs 'A' site.

No Travellers wanted the 'B' Site built so close to Cottingley 'A'. They also thought that it was too big and wanted smaller sites. The Travellers were pleased to have good amenity blocks like they had on the Cottingley 'A' site, but wished that it had been built somewhere else.

COTTINGLEY 'A' 1998

Cottingley 'B' Site

When Cottingley 'B' was opened in 1990, sixteen families came down from the old 'Top Site' on the hill, which had been closed. Twenty families joined them from the roadside camps around the city. Many families had not stopped together before and many moved off as they found the site too big and unsettling. Other families moved in to replace them and this process was repeated, so there was a high turnover of residents on the 'B' site compared to the older 'A' site.

PAINTED WAGON ON COTTINGLEY SPRINGS 'B' SITE IN 1992

This is Thomas and Bobby Doran with Kay Kay James in 1992 on Cottingley Springs 'B' site. The wagon is Blondie Tyres' and he was waiting to go on Lee Gap Fair. The wagon had just been made and it was all handpainted and done in gold.

Nora Doran

A BIG DAY FOR EVERYONE, WEDDING PARTY ON COTTINGLEY 'B', SUMMER 1994

It's in the morning time and all the children, the bridesmaids and pageboys, have got ready for Rosanne and Joe's wedding. They were over the moon 'cos it is a big event for children, to go to a wedding.

There's my Rocky, Billy Joe, Amber and Amos with their cousins Kelly, Miley, Jim, Sammy Joe and Bullerman.

Tina

COTTINGLEY 'B'

COUNCIL PROVISION

Crisis Time On Cottingley 'B'

During the 1990's many families were evicted from traditional stopping places in the city. They were relocated onto the Cottingley Springs 'B' site. Many of them did not want to come onto this large council site, but were given no choice. This again led to tensions and difficulties between families who had previously not stopped together and would have preferred to stay on their traditional camps. The Site went through a terrible time in 1996 and 1997. It became a virtual 'no-go-area' and many families left.

CHIDREN PLAYING, SUMMER 1998

Our grandchildren, Chelsea, Ellen and Jamie-Lee playing with Pa and Diane's daughter, Rebecca when it was hot last summer.   Margaret Joyce

CLEANING UP, SPRING 1999

That's me, washing down the slabs and little Kevin Price playing on his bike in the middle of the site. You can see the new fencing that the council have put around the slabs to mark out the spaces better.   Nolene Buxton

The council began to clear up and repair the damage. They decided to make the site smaller, in order to make it more manageable with fewer families living together.

In 1998 Cottingley Springs Caravan Site 'B' was reduced in size from thirty-six plots to twenty-six plots. There was no additional or alternative provision of sites made to compensate for this significant reduction in council facilities. At that time, the rent for a plot on the site at Cottingley was £60 per week for one caravan and £12 extra for a second caravan.

COTTINGLEY 'B'

An Uncertain Future On Cottingley 'B' Site

LOOKING AFTER EACH OTHER, COTTINGLEY 'B', SUMMER 1998

CHILDREN PLAYING TOGETHER ON COTTINGLEY 'B' SITE, SPRING 1999

That's my Rebecca and John with Lisa's Shanalis. They were playing around Lisa's plot. Rebecca was minding her and walking her round the site in the pushchair. This was taken last year in the middle of the summer 1998.

Diane Smith

That's Helen-Louise and Tammy Pattison, Samboy Lowther, Amos, Selena, Tom, Brian and Kelly Smith and Joe Moloney, all playin' together up and down the site. Families still come and go but there are some who have made it their permanent home now and it is much quieter on the site than it used to be.

Iggy Smith

There were further plans to build more Council Sites in the early nineties, when Leeds had a target of providing accommodation for another fifty families. These were never built, even though there was a 100% grant available to do so.

The duty to build Sites, and the 100% grant from the Department of the Environment to do so, were repealed under the 1994 Criminal Justice and Public Order Act.

Many families want alternative accommodation and some would like community housing, as developed in Ireland, and others would like smaller family sites.

COTTINGLEY 'B'

Index

of Contents by Topics and Subjects

Words and Pictures of Travelling Life

Index of Contents by Topics and Subjects

Words and Pictures of Travelling Life

Index of Contents by Topics and Subjects

Index of Contents by Topics and Subjects

Words and Pictures of Travelling Life

Index of Contents by Topics and Subjects

Words and Pictures of Travelling Life

Index

of Contents by Family Names

Words and Pictures of Travelling Life

Index of Contents by Family Names

Words and Pictures of Travelling Life

Index of Contents by Family Names

Words and Pictures of Travelling Life

Index of Contents by Family Names

Words and Pictures of Travelling Life

Index of Contents by Family Names

Index of Contents by Family Names

Index of Contents by Family Names

Words and Pictures of Travelling Life

Index of Contents by Family Names

Words and Pictures of Travelling Life

Review

Gypsies and Travellers in their own words

This is an important book. It is unusual and fascinating. From the mouths of Gypsies and Travellers we are told their own stories, stories which reveal many aspects of people whose lives have been a mystery on the margins of society, a people so often misunderstood and harshly judged. Accompanied by evocative photographs from personal collections, these stories tell of an unwritten England.

Taken from an oral culture, taped interviews have been written down in all their original and entertaining freshness. The questions have been removed so that they read like stories. They reveal a proud people struggling to come to terms with the enormity of societal upheaval during the last fifty years while at the same time trying to preserve their own traditions, language and crafts.

There is a sure poetry in Tilly Kelby's description of how difficult it sometimes is to live a settled life, when she explains how being settled can be unsettled. She declares,

"It's like a hunger - a longing comes over you. You just want to be away."

And oddly, for people always on the move, there is a strong sense of belonging, especially in the story of Bobby James who, without hesitation, says that,

"England is the prettiest piece of land on earth."

Many of the photographs reveal strong images of a bygone age for the people of the road. Sometimes they are poignant in depicting the hostile and difficult circumstances endured but they also reveal a resilience which today is being fully tested by all the new pressures of modern life that threaten the very existence of the Gypsies and Travellers.

When the children of Travellers go to school they are often singled out for rough justice by other children and they are subject to name calling and other types of bullying. The introduction of Council sites has helped alleviate some of the problems families face but the sense of being cooped up in confined space can sometimes give rise to tensions resulting from a lack of privacy. What comes through in all of these personal stories is the pride taken in the family and the strength which is drawn from that. Further strength is taken from their ancient languages of Romanes and Cant which ensure privacy of conversation.

Peter Saunders and his team have bothered to listen to and to ask questions of Gypsies and Travellers themselves. His team includes members of the Travelling Community; a sign of trust engendered in the completion of this most valuable piece of fieldwork about a people all too often misunderstood. This book points to a great wealth of information still waiting to be harvested of a folklore which could so easily be lost forever.

Michael Reeves
Poet and Broadcaster February 2000

Words and Pictures of Travelling Life